# —MASTERING THE ART OF—
# SUCCESS STRATEGIES

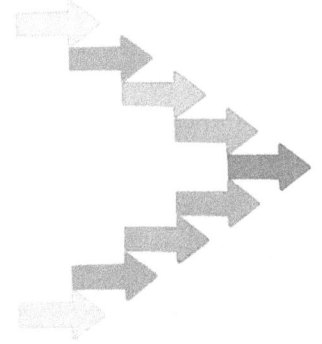

*Learn to Set Clear Goals, Craft Your Path to Achievement, Master Time Management, and Turn Your Dreams Into Reality*

by

## J P PATHAK

Email: jppathak1@gmail.com

Copyright © 2024 by J P Pathak

All rights reserved. No part of this book may be reproduced in any form without permission in writing from the author.

No part of this publication may be reproduced or transmitted in any form or by any means, mechanical or electronic, including photocopying or recording, by any information storage and retrieval system, or by email or any other means whatsoever without permission in writing from the author.

# DEDICATION

To *My Beloved Family,*

"This book is not just a product of my efforts but a reflection of the unwavering support and love you all have shown me.

Each page shows the encouragement, guidance, and inspiration you generously bestowed upon me throughout my journey.

To my Elder brother, Sh. Shrikrishna Ji, and my younger brothers Radharaman and Sukhdev, your presence in my life has been an anchor in times of uncertainty and a beacon of light in moments of darkness. Your unwavering support, sage advice, and boundless love have fuelled my determination and propelled me forward even when the path seemed daunting.

My Elder brother, Sh. Shrikrishna, your strength and wisdom have guided me, showing me the power of resilience and perseverance.

Radharaman and Sukhdev, your unwavering belief in me and your constant encouragement have inspired me, reminding me of the importance of courage and optimism.

As I embark on this chapter, I carry the lessons learned and the memories cherished with each of you by my side.

*This book is a testament to our shared journey, collective dreams, and the indomitable spirit of our family bond and values."*

With Love and Gratitude.

J P Pathak

# ACKNOWLEDGMENT

I want to express my sincere gratitude to everyone who contributed to the creation of this book.

I want to thank my family and friends for their unwavering support and encouragement throughout this journey. Your belief in me has been a constant source of inspiration.

I am deeply grateful to my coach and mentor, whose steadfast support and guidance have shaped my journey. With boundless patience and wisdom, you have nurtured my leadership qualities and encouraged me to strive for excellence. Even during moments of doubt, your belief in me has been a beacon of light, illuminating the path to personal and professional growth. Words cannot express my gratitude for your invaluable contribution to my life.

Thank you for believing in me and helping me become the best version of myself.

J P Pathak

# WHY IS THIS BOOK FOR YOU?

This book is an indispensable guide for leaders seeking to excel in today's competitive landscape. Through practical strategies and actionable insights, this book empowers readers to set clear goals, cultivate a growth mindset, overcome obstacles, and expand their sphere of influence.

Each Chapter explores essential topics and you will get a way forward for great success, such as

1- **Clear Goals Drive Success:** Setting clear, actionable goals are the foundation for achieving success.

2- **Resilience is Key:** Resilience allows leaders to overcome obstacles, adapt to change, and persevere through challenges,

3- **Adaptability Fuels Growth:** Embracing adaptability enables leaders to navigate uncertainty and capitalize on new opportunities.

4- **Continuous Learning Drives Excellence:** Committing to lifelong learning fosters personal and professional growth, enhancing leadership effectiveness.

5- **Networking Strengthens Connections:** Building strong networks fosters collaboration, support, and opportunities for growth and development.

6- **Celebrating Milestones Motivates:** Recognizing achievements boosts morale, fosters a positive culture, and reinforces progress toward goals.

**And more:**

Whether you are a seasoned sales leader or aspiring to climb the ranks, "Success Strategies for Sales Leaders" offers valuable guidance to help you achieve your professional goals and unlock your full potential. With a focus on personal development, team empowerment, and organizational success, this book serves as a comprehensive resource for anyone looking to thrive in the competitive world of sales leadership.

As you embark on your journey to success, may these strategies serve as your roadmap, guiding you towards greater achievements and fulfilment in your career.

Best wishes on your path to becoming a successful sales leader!

**With Regards,**

J P Pathak

# TABLE OF CONTENTS

**INTRODUCTION** ................................................................... **15**
    THE STORY OF RAMAYANA .................................................................. 17
    LEARNINGS FROM THIS MOMENT OF MEETING OF LORD RAMA WITH
    VIBHISHANA .................................................................................... 18

**SETTING CLEAR GOALS: DEFINING YOUR VISION FOR SUCCESS** ..... **21**
    STORYTIME ...................................................................................... 22
    VALUES ........................................................................................... 27
    LET US MOVE TO GOAL SETTING ....................................................... 27
    SELF-REFLECTION AND ASSESSMENT ................................................. 29
    EXERCISE: "GOAL TO RUN A MARATHON" ......................................... 30
    THE ART OF GOAL SETTING .............................................................. 33
    CHALLENGES AND OBSTACLES .......................................................... 34
    STORYTIME ...................................................................................... 35
    ENHANCED PRODUCTIVITY ............................................................... 36
    GREATER ACCOUNTABILITY .............................................................. 37
    SENSE OF ACHIEVEMENT .................................................................. 38
    CONTINUOUS IMPROVEMENT ........................................................... 39
    EXERCISE ........................................................................................ 40

**CRAFTING YOUR ACTION PLAN: TURNING DREAMS INTO REALITY . 41**
    IDENTIFYING YOUR GOALS ............................................................... 41
    SMART GOAL SETTING .................................................................... 42
    EXERCISE ........................................................................................ 42
    STORYTIME ...................................................................................... 45

## Overcoming Obstacles: Strategies For Resilience And Persistence ............... 47
### Storytime ............... 47
### Take Home Message ............... 49
### Introduction To Strategies For Resilience And Persistence ............... 51
### Storytime ............... 54

## Cultivating A Growth Mindset: Unlocking Your Full Potential ............... 57
### Storytime ............... 61
### Practical Tips To Cultivate A Growth Mindset ............... 64
### Growth Mindset In Action ............... 65
### Reflection And Action Planning ............... 66
### Exercise ............... 67
### Key Take-Home Messages ............... 68

## Mastering Time: "Strategies For Effective Time Management" ............... 71
### Storytime ............... 71
### Time Management Techniques ............... 79
### Fundamental Principles Of The GTD System ............... 83
### Case Study ............... 84
### Insight From An Expert ............... 85
### Summary ............... 85
### Building Resilient Habits: Sustaining Long-Term Success ............... 86

## Building Resilient Habits: Sustaining Long-Term Success 87
### Storytime ............... 87
### How To Develop Resilience? ............... 90

- Storytime ................................................................... 93
- Some Tips For Building Resilience ........................................... 94
- Real-Life Succes Story: Mona's Journey To Sales Excellence .................. 97
- Key Take-Home Messages ...................................................... 98

## Navigating Challenges: Strategies For Adaptability And Flexibility ......... 101

- Importance Of Adaptability And Flexibility ................................. 102
- Role Of Growth Mindset In Fostering Adaptability And Flexibility ........... 103
- Storytime .................................................................. 103
- Key Learnings From David's Experience ...................................... 104
- Practical Tips To Incorporate Flexibility Into Daily Routines And Decision-Making Processes .................................................. 105

## Expanding Your Sphere Of Influence: The Power Of Connections ............... 107

- How Can You Improve Networking? ............................................ 107
- Networking Action Plan ..................................................... 109

## Embracing Continuous Learning: Fueling Personal And Professional Growth .... 115

- Why Continuous Learning Matters For The Business ........................... 116
- The Value Of Continous Learning For Leaders ................................ 117
- Practical Tips For Continuous Learning ..................................... 118

## Celebrating Milestones: Recognizing Progress And Staying Motivated ......... 123

- Some Tips To Celebrate The Milestones And Success .......................... 125
- Reflection Question ........................................................ 126
- Exercise ................................................................... 126

STORYTIME ............................................................................... 128

**ABOUT THE AUTHOR** ........................................................ **131**

**OTHER BOOKS WRITTEN BY THE AUTHOR** ............................... **133**

**DISCLAIMER** ..................................................................... **135**

**MAY I ASK YOU A FAVOR?** ................................................... **137**

# INTRODUCTION

*"Strategy is about making choices, trade-offs; it's about deliberately choosing to be different."*

**- Micheal Porter**

Welcome to the next episode of the series Rise and Thrive. In the previous five episodes, we have enjoyed learning in the company of Ramdas, the central character in our series, and he will continue to be our guide in this episode as well. In the first five episodes, we have seen what 'The One Thing That Will Make You an Effective Leader' is and how to build on that strength discovered in the 1st episode. In subsequent episodes, we have seen the power of team building and goal Setting. Episode 5 was all about effective communication. We understand that communication is a vast topic and is difficult to define. We have learned how effective communication can help to improve our interpersonal skills, create meaningful connections, and handle communication challenges confidently and clearly. Let us move forward and walk into the next episode together.

Having spent decades in the sales profession, I have realized that only some achieve the same level of success despite putting in the same amount of hard work. This question has intrigued me since the beginning of my sales career. I was fortunate enough to have a good mentor who played a vital role in shaping my career. His interest in my enthusiasm and dedication has helped me become a champion in my field.

I learned that every step we take is guided by our choices in the journey toward success. Everybody has a right to choose, but you can exercise your choice only once, so be careful when making a choice next time. Why do I say that? These choices aren't merely random decisions but deliberate actions that shape our path and define our destination. As Michael Porter eloquently stated, "Strategy is about making choices and trade-offs; it's about deliberately choosing to be different."This sentiment encapsulates the essence of our quest for success, where each decision propels us forward on a unique trajectory toward our goals.

I want to share one incident that exemplifies the power of strategic choice and its impact on our journey.

One day, during a hot summer in my village, Ramdas came to his Guru JI with a serious question in his mind to ask him. His Guru Ji welcomed Ramdas with his known smile and offered him a glass of refreshing buttermilk. Once he settled with the coolness of buttermilk. Guru Ji asked Ramdas, why are you so severe today? What is in your mind? Ramdas grabbed the opportunity and jumped to use this opportunity. He asked Guru Ji, " Why do some individuals in our village possess more resources than others? Despite our collective toil and labor, disparities in wealth persist. What accounts for this disparity.?

In this exchange between Ramdas and his Guru Ji( Sage) lies a profound truth about the nature of success. As a curious boy, I learned that it is not merely the result of chance or circumstances but a product of deliberate choice and strategic action.

As we embark on our journey together, let us draw inspiration from this timeless tale and recognize that today's choices will shape our future.

Join me as we traverse the roadmap to success, exploring the strategies and insights that will guide us toward our goals.

Let us embrace the power of deliberate choice and chart a course toward a future defined by fulfillment and achievement.

### THE STORY OF RAMAYANA

Let me start with a reference from the epic Ramayana,

In the story of Ramayana, there is a significant moment when Vibhishana, the brother of Ravana, sends a message to Lord Rama asking for a meeting. Lord Rama's advisors suggest he should avoid meeting someone from the enemy's camp. Vibhishana still determines whether Lord Rama will accept him due to his association with Ravana. However, to everyone's surprise, Lord Rama warmly welcomes Vibhishana and addresses him as "Lankesh," which means "Lord of Lanka" or "King of Lanka."

Lord Rama then offers Vibhishana a seat next to his younger brother Laxman instead of in front of him, which is the first step he takes to give him importance in his camp despite his past allegiance to Ravana. This shows Lord Rama's kindness and ability to see beyond Vibhishana's affiliations, recognizing his sincerity and desire to do what is right.

After joining Lord Rama's side, Vibhishana is a valuable ally in the battle against Ravana. He provides crucial insights into Ravana's weaknesses and helps Lord Rama in his mission to rescue Sita and defeat the demon King. This moment highlights the themes of forgiveness, redemption, and the importance of making the right choices, even after past mistakes. It also emphasizes Lord Rama's qualities of compassion and fairness as a leader.

Similarly, in our quest for success, we are faced with moments of choice and transformation; like Vibhishana, we are called upon to summon the courage to seek guidance, embrace humility in our pursuit of knowledge, and align our actions with the principles of integrity and virtue.

## Learnings From This Moment Of Meeting Of Lord Rama With Vibhishana

1- **Leadership and compassion:** Lord Rama's leadership style emphasizes compassion and fairness, showing that authentic leadership involves understanding, acceptance, and empathy toward others.

2- **Recognition of Sincerity:** Lord Rama's acknowledgment of Vibhishana's sincerity demonstrates the value of recognizing and appreciating genuine intentions, even in unexpected circumstances.

3- **Second chance:** The moment underscores the idea that everyone deserves a second chance to make things right, regardless of their past actions or affiliations.

4- **Unity and cooperation:** Vibhishana's decision to switch sides and Lord Rama's acceptance of him highlights the importance of unity and cooperation in achieving common goals, even in the face of conflicts.

5- **Strength in Diversity:** Embracing Vibhishana despite his differences reinforces the idea that strength lies in diversity and inclusivity, as it allows for the pooling of talents, perspectives, and experiences toward a shared purpose.

These learnings are relevant in our professional life as well. As we embark on our journey, let us draw inspiration from the timeless wisdom of the Ramayana, recognizing that within its sacred verses lie timeless truths that illuminate the path toward success. Just as Vibhishana's journey led him to stand beside Lord Rama in his righteous quest, may our journey lead us towards fulfilling our aspirations and realizing our highest potential.

Let us move forward to define our vision for success.

Chapter #1

# SETTING CLEAR GOALS: DEFINING YOUR VISION FOR SUCCESS

*"Setting goals is the first step in turning the invisible into the visible."*

*- Tony Robbins*

Clarity of purpose is paramount in the journey towards success. Without a clear destination, we risk wandering amidst the myriad paths that stretch before us.

We will explore the transformative power of goal setting and delve into the strategies and techniques for setting goals that are not only SMART( Specific, Measurable, Achievable, Relevant, and Time-bound) but also aligned with our values, passion, and purpose. We will discuss the benefits of goal-setting, the challenges and obstacles we may encounter along the way, and the importance of accountability, support, and reflection in goal-setting.

Whether you are just starting in a leadership position or have already spent years in your role, if you are seeking to inspire and motivate your team, if you are an ambitious entrepreneur charting the course for your next venture, or simply a family man striving to live a life of purpose and meaning, you are invited to join us on this journey. Together, we will unlock the secrets to purposeful goal setting and discover the limitless potential within each of us to turn our dreams into reality.

What is the value of setting clear goals?

Setting clear goals provides a roadmap, guiding our actions and aligning our efforts towards a singular vision of achievement.

**STORYTIME**

I lived in Mumbai, the financial capital of India, for about a decade. I met many entrepreneurs and aspiring entrepreneurs there and learned many things from their experiences and aspirations. I had the opportunity to interact with Adarsh, a young entrepreneur with many ideas who is full of energy and desires to do something great and better than his family business.

I found him very ambitious and with a thrust of success. Adarsh found himself at a crossroads, unsure of the patch ahead. I sensed the need for direction for Adarsh and suggested a name that could mentor Adarsh to his father. Later, Adarsh and his father agreed to my suggestion, and Adarsh sought guidance from his mentor, a very seasoned professional. He imparted a simple yet profound lesson on setting clear goals. I am happy to share that Adarsh and his business are doing very well, and his company plans to launch an IPO soon.

I want to share one of my experiences with Adarsh and his mentor. It was a rainy day, and it was raining heavily. We had no option but to wait for the rain to stop. Adrash offered both of us a good, hot cup of coffee.

The mentor to Adarsh asked him, " Imagine yourself standing at the edge of a vast ocean "( we were near Juhu Beach, a very famous place in Mumbai), but you didn't have any map or compass; how will you navigate the waters before you?" before I could understand the situation, Adrash Said, Sir, I am recognizing the significance of having a clear destination in mind. The words of his mentor so inspired him that Adrash requested a special session. The mentor happily agreed to Adarsh's proposal. During that session, Adarsh defined his goals with clarity and precision. Adrash meticulously crafted a vision for his future, outlining specific milestones and objectives to guide his journey. That session is still fresh in my mind. Each goal was imbued with meaning and purpose, serving as a beacon of inspiration amidst the uncertainties of entrepreneurship. Each question from the Mentor gave Adarsh more clarity.

Adarsh made steady progress towards his goals as the days turned into weeks and months. With each step forward, he gained clarity and confidence, fueled by the knowledge that he was moving closer to his dreams.

I have closely seen Adarsh's progress and feel proud of him and his mentor.

The story of Adarsh serves as a testament to the transformative power of setting clear goals. Just as Adarsh navigated the waters of uncertainty with purpose and determination, we can chart our courses toward success by defining our goals with clarity and intention.

Remember:

*Clear Vision will guide our actions. Impossible becomes attainable. And the journey towards success becomes a path well-traveled.*

During a session between the Mentor and Adarsh, I noticed his mentor guided Adarsh to the following points.

1- **Define your Vision**: He repeatedly asked Adarsh to guide him by clarifying what success looks like for him. He helped Adarsh envision his ideal future and identify the key milestones he needed to achieve.

2- **Be specific**: Set clear, measurable goals that are specific and actionable. Break down larger goals into smaller, manageable tasks to make them more attainable.

3- **Prioritize**: Focus on goals that align with your values and long-term objectives. Prioritize your goals based on their importance and relevance to your overall vision.

4- **Create a Plan**: Develop a strategic plan outlining the steps you need to take to achieve each goal. Set deadlines and milestones to track your progress along the way.

5- **Stay Flexible**: Be open to adjusting your goals as circumstances change. Adaptability is critical to overcoming obstacles and staying on course towards success.

I learned that your vision should be inspiring, specific, and aligned with your values and long-term objectives.

Let me share some examples of defining a vision:

If you are a Sales Representative, then you need to have a **'Career Vision'** and vision statement could be

*"My goal is to become a respected leader in the pharmaceutical industry ( Or any Industry you are in), known for my innovative ideas and transformative impact on the organization."*

Suppose you have a vision for personal growth. In that case, you want to live a purposeful and fulfilling life, constantly striving for self-improvement and embracing new experiences that broaden your horizons.

If you come from a family of entrepreneurs or aspire to start your own business, you may have an "Entrepreneurial Vision." This means you want to create a successful business that addresses a significant market issue, provides value to customers, and generates sustainable growth and profits.

If you are married or planning to get married, you can create a **'Family Vision'** statement. For example, it could read, 'To foster a loving and supportive family environment where every member is valued, respected, and empowered to pursue their dreams.'

If you are a social worker or a politician, your **'Community Vision'** Statement could be: "To contribute to the betterment of my community by volunteering my time and resources to causes that promote social justice, equality, and environmental sustainability. "

One of the world's issues today is health and wellness, and everyone must have a vision. The vision statement could be: "To prioritize my physical and mental well-being by adopting a balanced lifestyle that includes regular exercise, healthy eating habits, and mindfulness practices."

Human beings have four basic desires-

We have covered three basic needs: health, Happiness, success, and financial independence. We also need a vision statement for the fourth desire because desires are usually weak and need support.

So the **'Financial Vision'** Statement is here: to achieve financial independence and security by saving and investing wisely, building multiple streams of passive income, and living within my means.

"Defining a vision involves articulating your aspirations and desired outcomes. It should be inspiring, specific, and aligned with your values and long-term objectives."

Since vision has to be aligned with values, let us understand the meaning of values.

## Values

"*Success in sales comes from integrity, authenticity, and a genuine desire to help others succeed*"- Unknown.

In today's dynamic sales world, success is often equated with numbers and your daily or monthly quotas. Do you agree?

True success goes beyond closing deals; it's about building lasting relationships based on trust and mutual respect. **Integrity, authenticity, and a genuine desire to help others succeed** distinguish top-performing sales professionals from the rest. For example, imagine a sales representative who prioritizes the needs of their clients above all else; instead of pushing products or services for the sake of meeting targets, they take the time to understand their clients' challenges, offer tailored solutions, and provide ongoing support and guidance. By consistently demonstrating these values in their interactions, they earn their client's trust and loyalty and achieve long-term career success.

## Let Us Move To Goal Setting

Few things are as fundamental as setting clear and meaningful goals in the pursuit of success and personal fulfillment. Tony Robbins's above statement underscores the transformative power of goal setting, highlighting its ability to transform dreams and aspirations into tangible reality.

It is essential to have Goals in our life. Goals are like a roadmap that guides our actions, providing direction and purpose in our journey towards achievement.

Without clear goals, we risk drifting aimlessly, without a sense of purpose or direction. Goals give us something to strive for, a target to aim at, and a compelling reason to push beyond our comfort zone.

The purpose of goal setting begins with introspection and self-reflection. It requires us to identify our values, passions, strengths, and weaknesses and align our goals with our aspirations and core beliefs. Setting goals that resonate with our deepest desires and motivations increases our chances of success and fulfillment.

Once we have defined our goals, breaking them down into smaller, achievable steps is crucial. These milestones act as checkpoints along our journey, enabling us to assess our progress and make necessary adjustments. Regular review and evaluation of our goals ensure we remain committed to our vision despite obstacles and setbacks. Goal setting is a powerful tool that helps us grow personally and professionally. It empowers us to **dream big**, take action, and create the life we desire.

Remember:

"Set clear and meaningful goals and stay committed to unlock the full potential and turn your dreams into reality."

We know that our goals should be SMART, and we should follow the **Goal-Setting Process.**

## Self-Reflection And Assessment

Begin by reflecting on your values, passions, strengths, and weaknesses. Consider what truly matters to you and what you want to achieve in various areas of your life.

**Define Your Vision:**

Envision your ideal future and identify specific outcomes you want to achieve. Your goals should inspire, motivate, and align with your values and long-term objectives.

**Set SMART Goals:**

S-Specific

M-Measurable

A-Achievable

R-Relevant and

T-Time-bound

**Prioritize Your Goals:**

Determine which goals are most important and relevant to your overall vision. Focus your time and energy on goals that will impact your life most and align with your values and aspirations.

**Create an Action Plan:**

Develop a strategic plan outlining the steps you need to take to achieve each goal. Set deadlines and milestones to track your progress and hold yourself accountable.

**Be Flexible:**

Be open to adjusting your goals and action plans as circumstances change. Life is unpredictable, and unexpected challenges may arise along the way. Stay flexible and resilient, and be willing to adapt your approach as needed.

**Review the Progress:**

Review your goals and assess your progress regularly. Celebrate your success and learn from any setbacks or obstacles you encounter. Use feedback to refine your goals and action plan and stay focused on moving forward.

**Stay Motivated and Persistent:**

Stay motivated by keeping your vision and goals at the forefront of your mind. Surround yourself with supportive people, seek inspiration from others who have achieved similar goals, and remain steadfast in your endeavors, even when faced with challenges.

**EXERCISE: "GOAL TO RUN A MARATHON"**

Make SMART Goal

Hint: Marathon is 42.195 Km

Time Horizon: For example, if the next marathon is in the city ( Name )..... on May ( Month) 20th ( Date)in 2025(year), you have 12 months to prepare.

How many hours do you want to finish the marathon (Specifically) in under 4 hours?

Break down into Smaller, Actionable Steps:

    Step 1- Baseline Fitness Level-

    Step 2 Training plan-

    Step 3 Regular Running Routine-

    Step 4 Strength Training and Cross Training-

    Step 5 Progress Monitoring and Adjust Training-

    Step 6 Half-Marathon Milestone-

    Step 7 Diet and Hydration Plan-

    Step 8 Final Day Preparation

Action Plan:

Schedule fitness assessment with a personal trainer (Mention Date)

Research and consult with a running coach to develop a training plan( Mention Date)

Begin regular running routine daily for 45 min ( Starting Date)

Incorporate Strength and cross-training sessions into a weekly routine( Starting Date)

Monitor Weekly Progress and keep records (Weekly)

Register and complete the half marathon race(Date)

Appointment with Nutritionist and getting fueling plan( Mention Date) and Finally

Finalize race-day preparations and logistics( Marathon Date)

By breaking down the SMART goal of running a marathon into smaller, actionable steps and creating an action plan with specific deadlines, you can systematically work towards achieving your goal while staying focused and motivated throughout the process.

Using a specific framework, you can create SMART goals. This method can be applied to personal, professional, or financial goals.

Remember:

"When setting goals, it's important to be Specific, Measurable, Achievable, Relevant, and Time-bound. To achieve this, brainstorming, prioritizing, and breaking down goals into actionable steps can be helpful."

Setting goals is an invaluable skill; anyone can learn and grow from it, so start making SMART Goals for your growth.

## The Art Of Goal Setting

**Benefits of Goal-Setting**: There are many benefits of setting SMART goals, such as Increased motivation, improved focus, enhanced productivity, and a greater possibility of success.

- **A-** Increased Motivation- Setting clear, achievable goals can boost motivation by providing a sense of purpose and direction. For example, a sales team may set a goal to increase monthly revenue by 10%. With this target in mind, team members are motivated to work harder and smarter to achieve the desired outcome.

- **B-** Improved Focus and Clarity- Goal setting helps individuals and teams prioritize tasks and allocate resources effectively. For example, a project manager may set specific milestones and deadlines for completing key deliverables, ensuring everyone is on the same page and working towards a common objective.

- **C-** Enhanced Productivity- With well-defined goals, individuals can better manage their time and resources, increasing productivity. For example, a business head may set a goal to launch a new product within six months. This goal serves as a roadmap, guiding the head's actions and decisions to meet the deadline effectively.

- **D-** Greater Accountability- Goal setting encourages accountability by setting clear expectations and measuring progress against predetermined benchmarks. For instance, a student may set a goal to achieve a certain grade point average by the end of the semester. By regularly monitoring their performance and seeking feedback, students hold themselves accountable for their academic success.

E- Sense of Achievement—Accomplishing goals provides a sense of achievement and satisfaction, boosting self-confidence and self-esteem. For example, an individual who sets a goal to run a marathon and crosses the finish line experiences a profound sense of accomplishment, knowing they have overcome challenges and achieved something meaningful.

F- Continuous Improvement- Goal setting fosters a culture of continuous improvement by encouraging individuals and teams to set increasingly ambitious goals over time. For example, a software development team may set a goal to release a new version of their product with enhanced features and functionality every month. This iterative approach drives innovation and growth within the organization.

**CHALLENGES AND OBSTACLES**

*"Obstacles don't have to stop you. If you run into a wall, don't turn around and give up. Figure out how to climb it, go through it, or work around it."*

*- Michael Jordan*

Goal setting is not without challenges and obstacles. Many barriers to goal achievement exist, such as lack of clarity, procrastination, fear of failure, and external constraints.

## STORYTIME

In a previous episode, you met Sunny ( Son of one of Friends), a software engineer based in Bengaluru, India. Sunny was tasked with leading a team to develop a new app within a tight deadline. Throughout the project, Sunny set his sights on some ambitious goals. He aimed to deliver a high-quality app that would meet all user needs and exceed the client's expectations.

As the project progressed, Sunny encountered some significant obstacles, including narrow timelines, technical complexities, and ever-changing client requirements. These challenges threatened the project's success, and despite Sunny's best efforts, he found himself overwhelmed and uncertain about how to proceed.

To overcome these challenges, Sunny turned to his team for support and suggestions. Together, they brainstormed solutions, prioritized tasks, and adapted their approach to meet the project's evolving needs. Through collaboration and perseverance, they overcame obstacles and delivered the app on time and within budget.

Sunny's story highlights the importance of resilience and adaptability in facing challenges and obstacles. Like Sunny, we, as Individuals and teams, often encounter unexpected hurdles that threaten our progress toward our goals. These can be tight timelines, resource constraints, or unforeseen circumstances; challenges are inevitable in any endeavor.

The above quote from Michael Jordan suggests that obstacles should not be viewed as insurmountable barriers but rather as opportunities for growth and innovation. Instead of turning back or giving up in the face of adversity, individuals can adopt a proactive mindset and seek creative solutions to overcome challenges.

Sunny and his team display resilience by remaining focused on their goal and working together to find alternative approaches to address their obstacles.

Remember: "Embracing flexibility and adaptability helps navigate challenges and achieve success.."

## Enhanced Productivity

*"The way to get started is to quit talking and begin doing."*

*- Waly Disney*

Productivity is critical to the success of any project. To maximize productivity, you must implement several strategies, including setting clear goals, delegating tasks effectively ( you should know what can be delegated and to whom), and leveraging technology to streamline workflow. Establishing daily or weekly meetings (Depending on the type of project), prioritizing tasks, and providing ongoing feedback and support to the team members will help you create a culture of accountability and collaboration that will foster productivity.

Despite facing unexpected challenges and setbacks, such as budget constraints and last-minute client requests, Sunny and his team remain focused and resilient. Through their collective efforts and commitment to excellence, they can deliver the app ahead of schedule and exceed the client's expectations.

Remember: "Take action and move forward with purpose."

## GREATER ACCOUNTABILITY

*"Accountability breeds response-ability."*

*- Stephen Covey*

Imagine you are a sales manager whose team is responsible for achieving monthly sales targets. You should know that accountability is essential to your success. To foster a culture of accountability, you should set clear expectations, track performance metrics, and provide regular feedback and support to your team members. Each team member is to be assigned specific sales goals. Hold regular review meetings and conduct a performance review to ensure that each team member is aware of their responsibilities and is accountable for their performance.

Challenges like market fluctuations and intense competition may occur, but your team should remain committed to achieving their goals. You can help your team achieve the goal through open communication, collaboration, and a shared sense of purpose.

Remember; "It is your responsibility to hold team members accountable for their individual and collective success.."

## SENSE OF ACHIEVEMENT

*"The only limit to our realization of tomorrow will be our doubts of today."*

*- Franklin D Roosevelt*

In the previous episode, I shared a story about my childhood friend. His journey has been filled with challenges and setbacks. He lost his father at a young age, and his mother, with the help of his uncle, managed to support his education. His uncle also helped him set up a business. His determination to pursue his dream paid dividends; today, he is a respected businessman. He takes pride in overcoming adversity and staying true to his vision. His determination turned his dream into reality. The satisfaction and fulfillment he experiences from achieving his goal fuel his passion and drive for future success.

Remember: "With Determination, perseverance, and a positive mindset, you can overcome any obstacle and achieve your goals."

## Continuous Improvement

*"Success is not final, failure is not fatal: It is the courage to continue that count."*

*- Winston Churchill*

We have met Ramdas, a lifelong learner committed to personal and professional development. Ramdas sets a goal to learn a new skill each month, whether mastering a new language, acquiring a new hobby, or gaining expertise in a specific interest. Through your dedication to continuous improvement, you can expand your knowledge, enhance your ability, and broaden your horizons, like Ramdas.

Balancing work, family, and personal commitment may be challenging, but you must remain focused on your goal of continuous learning.

It would be best to push yourself outside of your comfort zone. Each new skill you learn will make you more confident.

Summary:

In this chapter, we have explored the transformative power of goal-setting and its impact on personal and professional success. We have discussed the benefits of setting SMART goals, including increased motivation, improved focus, enhanced productivity, greater accountability, a sense of achievement, and continuous improvement.

Through stories, quotes, and discussions, we have seen how individuals have leveraged goal-setting to overcome challenges, achieve their dreams, and unlock their full potential. Goal-setting provides a roadmap for success and empowers individuals to turn their aspirations into reality.

**EXERCISE**

Can you please reflect on your goals and aspirations and consider how you can apply the principles of goal-setting to achieve them?

Setting clear, purposeful goals and taking decisive action toward attainment can create a life of meaning, fulfillment, and success.

Let's discuss the action plan."**Taking Steps Towards Success."**

## Chapter #2

# CRAFTING YOUR ACTION PLAN: TURNING DREAMS INTO REALITY

*"The journey of a thousand miles begins with a single step."*

*- Lao Tzu*

Embarking on a new journey or pursuing our goals and aspirations can be intimidating, especially when taking that first step. However, as Lao Tzu once said, every incredible journey begins with that initial, courageous stride forward. This chapter will delve into the transformative power of action planning, which involves a systematic approach to turning our dreams into reality through discussions, purposeful steps, and implementation.

### IDENTIFYING YOUR GOALS

It is essential to have a clear destination in mind before embarking on any personal or professional journey. In some cases, it may be a combination of both. What will make a difference? Your values, passion, and long-term aspirations will make a big difference. By identifying your goals, you will clarify what truly matters to you and what you hope to achieve in the months and years ahead.

## SMART Goal Setting

Once you identify your goals, the next step is transforming them into SMART goals.

Setting clear, well-defined objectives will lay the foundation for a successful action plan that guides you toward your desired outcomes.

In my professional life, I met many people and had the opportunity to interact with them closely. Many of them could not tell me what they wanted to achieve. Some were struggling to follow the process of identifying their goals. I tried to help them uncover their deepest desires, aspirations, and ambitions.

I always suggest that people follow certain things.

A- **Reflect on Your Values and Passions**

B- **Clarify Your Vision for the Future**

C- **Set Short-Term and Long-Term goals**

D- **Consider Different Areas of Your Life**

E- **Prioritize Your Goals**

F- **Always Have Written Goals**

**EXERCISE**

Reflect on what truly matters to you in life.

What are your core values, Beliefs, and Principles?

Why should we consider Values, Beliefs, and Principles in identifying our goals?

Our **Values, beliefs**, and **principles** often serve as guiding forces in our lives, shaping the goals we set and the actions we take. By exploring these aspects of ourselves, we can better understand what truly matters to us and align our goals accordingly.

Reflecting values, beliefs, and principles can provide **clarity** and **direction** when identifying goals. It helps us discern which goals are most meaningful and relevant to our identity and purpose, thus enhancing our motivation and commitment to achieving them.

When goals are aligned with values, beliefs, and principles, we are more likely to experience a sense of **authenticity** and **fulfillment** as we pursue them. This alignment fosters a greater sense of purpose and satisfaction, enhancing overall well-being and life satisfaction.

Remember: "Set goals that resonate with who you are and what they stand for."

Let us break down **Values, Beliefs,** and **Principles.**

**Values:** Values are deeply held beliefs about what is essential or desirable. They serve as guiding principles that influence our attitudes, behaviors, and decisions. Values can encompass various concepts, such as honesty, integrity, compassion, fairness, freedom, family, and community. They reflect what we consider morally right or wrong and shape our priorities and preferences in life.

Example: Consider someone who values honesty. They prioritize truthfulness and transparency in their interactions with others and strive to act with integrity in all aspects of their lives, even when faced with difficult choices.

**Beliefs**:

Beliefs are convictions or acceptances that something is true or exists, often based on personal experiences, cultural influences, or learned teachings. Beliefs can be about oneself, others, the world, or higher powers. They influence our perceptions, interpretations, and judgments of reality, shaping how we understand and make sense of the world.

Example: A person who believes in the power of hard work and perseverance approaches challenges with a mindset of resilience and optimism, viewing diligent effort and determination as essential for success.

**Principles**:

Principles are fundamental truths or rules that govern behavior and decision-making. They represent core ideals or standards that guide our conduct and interactions with others. Principles often derive from values and beliefs, serving as practical guidelines for ethical and moral conduct. They help individuals navigate complex situations and make ethical choices following their values.

Example: One common principle is the Golden Rule: "Treat others as you would like to be treated." This principle emphasizes the importance of empathy, kindness, and respect in interpersonal relationships, encouraging individuals to consider the perspectives and feelings of others in their interactions.

### STORYTIME

### The Compassionate Leader'

In my hometown, a highly respected business leader named Keshav was known for his unwavering commitment to his values and principles. Keshav firmly believed in the importance of hard work and perseverance and held a firm conviction that determined efforts were crucial for success.

One day, Keshav faced a difficult decision: his company faced financial difficulties, and layoffs seemed inevitable to keep the business afloat. While some may prioritize profit above all else, Keshav's principles guided him to consider the well-being of his employees above everything else.

Keshav took a different approach based on his belief in hard work and perseverance. He gathered his team and openly discussed the situation, expressing his concern for their welfare and inviting their input on potential solutions. Together, they brainstormed creative strategies to minimize layoffs, such as implementing cost-saving measures and reallocating resources.

Keshav's commitment to his values and principles inspired his employees to stand behind him, creating a culture of trust, collaboration, and resilience within the company. Despite their challenges, Ramdas and his team emerged more vital than ever, united by a shared belief in the transformative power of hard work, perseverance, and compassion.

Some key takeaways from the story of Ramdas:

1. **The power of Values**: Stay true to your values even when making difficult decisions.

2. **Leadership with Empathy**: Keshav demonstrated compassionate leadership by prioritizing his employees' well-being and fostering open communication and collaboration, creating a supportive and resilient organizational culture from which we can learn.

3. **Resilience in Adversity**: In times of crisis, Keshav's resilience and optimism were instrumental in navigating challenges and finding innovative solutions. His belief in the power of hard work and perseverance empowered him and his team to overcome obstacles and emerge stronger than before.

4. **The Importance of Collaboration**: Keshav encouraged collective problem-solving and decision-making, leading to better outcomes for all.

5. **Leading by Example**: Keshav's leadership actions spoke volumes about his character and integrity.

Remember: "Stay true to your principles."

## Chapter #3

## OVERCOMING OBSTACLES: STRATEGIES FOR RESILIENCE AND PERSISTENCE

*"Adversity introduces a man to himself."*

**- Albert Einstein**

I want to share two stories with you. One story is from the epic Mahabharata, and the other is from the real world. Both these stories have a positive message that will inspire us to face any challenges that come our way with confidence. Let's remember that obstacles are meant to be overcome.

**STORYTIME**

In the epic Mahabharata, the character of Arjuna faces many challenges during his journey. Several instances in the epic depict his struggles. One such incident occurs during the battle of Kurukshetra, where Arjuna finds himself overwhelmed with doubt and despair on the battlefield. Faced with the prospect of fighting his kin, he turns to his charioteer, Lord Krishna, seeking guidance and clarity.

With his divine wisdom, Krishna imparts to Arjuna the teachings of the Bhagavad Gita, emphasizing the significance of duty, righteousness, and resilience in the face of adversity. Through their conversation, Arjuna learns to overcome his fear and doubts, finding the strength and courage to fulfill his responsibilities as a warrior.

Let us learn from the conversation between Arjuna and Lord Krishna:

1- Resilience is a skill: Resilience is a skill that can be developed through a growth mindset, viewing challenges as opportunities for growth.

2- Adaptability is Key: Being open-minded, exploring alternatives, and adapting to change is crucial to overcoming obstacles.

3- Perseverance pays: Success often requires perseverance, especially when facing adversity. Stay committed to your goals and persist through setbacks.

4- Learn and Grow: Every obstacle presents an opportunity for learning and growth. Learn from every experience and seek feedback.

5- Seek Support: Whenever you face obstacles, don't hesitate to seek help from your mentor, colleagues, friends, or family. They can encourage and support you.

Let me share another story: Bachendri Pal's Everest Ascent.

Bachendri Pal was born into a modest family in Uttarakhand, India. Despite facing financial constraints, she bored a deep-seated dream of scaling the world's highest peak—Mount Everest. Bachendri's passion for mountaineering immersed her in rigorous training and preparation. Despite being the only woman in her course, she refused to be intimidated by the physical and mental challenges ahead.

In 1984, Bachendri Pal embarked on her historic expedition to Mount Everest as part of an Indian woman's team. The journey was fraught with complex conditions, including treacherous terrain, extreme weather, and altitude sickness. However, Bachendri's unresolute resolve and resilience propelled her forward, and she overcame each obstacle with determination and grit.

On May 23, 1984, BAchendri Pal achieved her lifelong dream, becoming the first Indian Woman to reach the summit of Mount Everest. Her triumphant ascent made history and inspired countless individuals- men and women- to pursue their dreams, no matter how daunting the obstacles may seem.

### TAKE HOME MESSAGE

1. **Dream Big, Start Small**: Bachendri Pal had a simple dream and a passion for mountaineering that led her to Everest. She turned her dreams into reality by setting ambitious goals and taking incremental steps.

2. **Resilience in the Face of Adversity**: Bachendri Pal encountered numerous obstacles on her journey, from physical barriers to societal barriers. However, her resilience and determination enabled her to persevere through adversity and ultimately reach the summit of Everest.

3. **Believe in Yourself**: Despite skepticism and doubt from others, Bachendri Pal remained steadfast in her belief in herself and her abilities. Confidence is a powerful force that can propel anyone to pursue their goals.

4. **Inspire Others**: Bachendri Pal's ascent of Mount Everest inspired countless individuals worldwide. She paved the way for others to believe in themselves and strive for greatness.

Each obstacle encountered on Bachendri Pal's journey served as an opportunity for growth and learning.

"Embrace challenges with courage and resilience."

There are many more stories around us to learn from.

The story of Oprah Winfrey is another example from the real world. She faced numerous obstacles on her path to success. Born into poverty in rural Mississippi, Oprah endured a challenging childhood marked by poverty, abuse, and hardship. Despite these early setbacks, she possessed an innate drive and resilience that propelled her towards her goals.

In her early career, Oprah faced rejection and discrimination as she pursued opportunities in the media industry; she was told that she was not fit for television and faced skepticism about her ability to connect with audiences. However, Oprah refused to be deterred by these obstacles. She continued to pursue her passion for broadcasting, honing her skills as a journalist and talk show host.

In 1986, Oprah launched "The Winfrey Show," a groundbreaking talk show that would become one of television's most successful and influential programs. Oprah's authenticity, empathy, and resilience resonated with viewers worldwide. Through her show, she tackled various issues, from personal development and empowerment to social justice and philanthropy, inspiring millions to overcome obstacles and pursue their dreams.

The above stories demonstrate that overcoming obstacles is not only possible but achievable with the right mindset, determination, and perseverance.

Remember: "Every obstacle presents an opportunity for learning and growth. So Learn and Grow"

## INTRODUCTION TO STRATEGIES FOR RESILIENCE AND PERSISTENCE

In the face of life's inevitable challenges and setbacks, the ability to bounce back, persevere, and thrive is invaluable. Let us explore strategies for resilience and persistence- two essential qualities that empower us to overcome adversity and achieve our goals.

What is Resilience?

Resilience can be defined as the capacity to recover quickly from difficulties. It involves adapting positively to adversity, maintaining a sense of perspective, and moving forward despite obstacles.

What is Persistence?

Persistence is continuing to pursue one's goals despite facing obstacles, failures, or setbacks.

We will discuss the strategies and techniques we can employ to cultivate resilience and persistence. Drawing inspiration from real-life stories of resilience, such as those of Oprah Winfrey, Ramdas, and Bachendri Pal, we will explore practical tips and exercises to help us navigate challenges with confidence and courage.

Suppose you are going through a tough time in your personal life or career or facing unexpected challenges. In that case, the strategies mentioned here will help you overcome adversity, stay focused on your goals, and emerge stronger. Make resilience and persistence your guiding principles in your journey to navigate life's ups and downs with determination and unwavering resolve.

We will discuss actionable strategies you can implement daily to enhance your resilience and persistence, From developing a positive mindset and building strong support networks to practicing self-care and setting realistic goals.

These tips empower you to face adversity and emerge more vital than ever.

Insight:

One critical insight into resilience is the importance of reframing challenges as opportunities for growth. Instead of viewing setbacks as insurmountable obstacles, resilient people see them as valuable learning experiences that can strengthen their skills, character, and resilience.

Adopt a growth mindset. Cultivate resilience and bounce back stronger than before.

Exercise:

Take a few moments and think of a recent challenge or setback you have faced in your life.

Write down the details of the situation.

Can you reframe this challenge as an opportunity for growth and learning?

Hint: ask yourself what lessons you can learn from experience.

How can I use this setback to strengthen my skills?

What opportunities for growth does this challenge present?

Then:

Please write down your reflections on a piece of paper, diary, or notebook, focusing on the positive aspects of the situation and opportunities it offers for personal development.

This is the time to brainstorm concrete steps to apply these lessons to future challenges, setting goals and action plans to help you navigate adversity with resilience and determination.

My Practical tip suggestion is :

Cultivate a strong support network of friends, family, mentors, and colleagues who can provide emotional support, encouragement, and guidance during difficult times.

Feel free to ask for support when you need it the most.

Face challenges with confidence.

### STORYTIME

Let me share a real-time life story,

One of my friend's sons works at a large IT company in Bengaluru. He faced a significant setback early in his career while trying to secure a major client he had been working with for months. Despite his hard work, he encountered multiple rejections that left him disheartened and uncertain about his prospects. Concerned about the impact on his confidence and future assignments, Arab turned to his father, a trusted mentor, for guidance.

He shared his experience with his father, who suggested that he should reframe the situation as an opportunity for growth and learning. He asked his son to recall the feedback he received from his client and identify areas where he could improve his sales pitch, communication, and product knowledge to meet his client's needs better. My friend also advised his son to seek constructive feedback from his sales manager and colleagues on enhancing his sales approach.

With renewed determination and a growth mindset, Arab (my friend's son) developed a plan to address the areas of improvement identified through the feedback process. He invested time and effort into refining his sales techniques, practicing his sales pitch, and expanding his product knowledge.

Over time, Arab's resilience and persistence paid off as he saw positive results in his sales efforts. He secured new clients, closed deals, and built more robust customer relationships. By proactively overcoming setbacks and embracing challenges as opportunities for growth, Arab strengthened his resilience and achieved tremendous success in his sales career. Today, he is working as a team leader.

Remember: "Adopt a positive mindset and seek opportunities for learning and development."

Recap:

In the previous chapters, we have explored essential aspects of personal and professional development, from setting clear goals and crafting action plans to overcoming obstacles with resilience and persistence. By defining our vision for success, taking concrete steps toward our goals, and navigating challenges with courage and determination, we have laid the groundwork for growth and achievement.

As we continue our journey of self-discovery and empowerment, we focus on the power of mindset in shaping our experiences and outcomes. In the next chapter, "Cultivating a Growth Mindset: Unlocking Your Full Potential," we will delve into the transformative concept of a growth mindset—a belief system that fosters resilience, learning, and innovation.

We will explore how to cultivate a growth mindset and harness its power to thrive in an ever-changing world.

Join us as we embark on self-discovery and personal growth, exploring the mindset shifts that can unlock new possibilities and propel us toward tremendous success and fulfillment.

Chapter #4

# CULTIVATING A GROWTH MINDSET: UNLOCKING YOUR FULL POTENTIAL

*"The only way to do great work is to love what you do."*

*- **Steve Jobs***

During a session, one of my participants asked me what the most powerful tool at our disposal is. The CEO hired me to work on people development because the company needed help to grow. My friend, a respected coach in the industry, shared this insight with me. Out of curiosity, I asked my friend what his response was. He said the lens through which we perceive the world and interpret our experiences is the most powerful tool. I was intrigued and asked him to explain this further. He told me his response to the participant was, "One of the most powerful tools at our disposal is our mindset." This mindset is a lens through which we view the world. It is based on our fundamental beliefs about our abilities, talents, and potential for growth.

We will explore the concept of a growth mindset- a belief system that views challenges, setbacks, and failures as opportunities for learning and growth.

What is the difference between a fixed mindset and a growth mindset?

While a fixed mindset sees intelligence and talent as static traits, a growth mindset embraces the idea that our abilities can be developed through dedication, effort, and resilience.

Cultivating a growth mindset is not just about adopting a positive attitude or thinking optimistically; it's about embracing a deeper understanding of the learning process and our capacity for improvement.

"To overcome obstacles with resilience and achieve greater success and fulfillment in your life- Foster a growth mindset."

Is it that easy to practice? I asked my friend.

His response gave me confidence. He shared the principles of a growth mindset and practical strategies for cultivating it. He also gave real-life examples of those who have embraced this mindset to achieve extraordinary success.

I have a story about an organization struggling due to its employees' fixed mindset. However, the CEO strongly believed in his ability and refused to be discouraged. He viewed every obstacle as an opportunity for learning and growth. With perseverance and a belief in his ability to learn and improve, the CEO achieved his goals and built a thriving business empire from scratch. When I requested him to share the beginning of his journey with his team, he started with the story of Thomas Edison, the light bulb inventor. Edison famously said, "I have not failed. I have found 10,000 ways that won't work." This inspired people with Edison's resilience and persistence in the face of failure. The CEO and his team then embarked on a journey to cultivate a growth mindset.

Through perseverance and a belief in his ability to learn and improve, the CEO eventually achieved his goals, building a growing business with satisfied and happy employees.

This story is a reminder of the transformative power of a growth mindset.

Remember: "Maintain a belief in your capacity for growth."

I encourage you to adopt a growth mindset to learn and grow.

### 1- Embrace Challenges:

One of the fundamental principles of a growth mindset is the willingness to embrace challenges as opportunities for growth and learning instead of avoiding complex tasks or shying away from obstacles. Always approach them with curiosity and enthusiasm. Every challenge allows you to stretch your abilities, develop new skills, and expand your knowledge.

Remember: " By Confronting challenges head-on, you will gain a deeper understanding of your strength and capabilities."

### 2- Efforts are the Foundation for success:

Mastery and success are the results of consistent effort and perseverance over time. Don't rely solely on natural talent or innate abilities; you must recognize the value of hard work, dedication, and deliberate practice in achieving your goals.

Put the time and effort required to improve your skills and overcome obstacles.

Remember: "Progress is a journey marked by incremental gains and continuous learning."

### 3- Learn from Feedback:

Those with a growth mindset see feedback as a valuable source of information and an opportunity for growth. These people take even negative feedback positively.

Every feedback gives you another chance to learn, adapt, and improve. Be proactive in seeking feedback and welcome constructive criticism. You can use such information to refine your approach and enhance the performance.

Remember: Welcome! Feedback is a catalyst for growth. Seek feedback to become a better version of yourself.

### 4- Cultivate Resilience:

Resilience is a vital trait of individuals who possess a growth mindset. It allows them to recover and keep going despite obstacles and difficulties. It's important to remember that setbacks are temporary and can provide opportunities for learning and growth. Instead of dwelling on problems, always focus on finding solutions. Even when faced with obstacles, stay committed to your goals.

Remember: "Develop resilience to overcome challenges and achieve success."

## 5- Celebrate Growth and Progress:

People with a growth mindset celebrate every success, whether small or big. They feel proud of themselves before major milestones or achievements.

They acknowledge and appreciate the progress they make along the way. They recognize that growth is a continuous journey marked by small victories and increments, and they take pride in their efforts and accomplishments.

Remember: "Stay motivated, inspired, and committed to your personal and professional development."

The principles of a growth mindset can help you unlock your full potential and achieve tremendous success and fulfillment in life. By embracing and practicing these principles, you can develop a mindset of growth, resilience, and possibility. This mindset empowers you to overcome obstacles, reach your goals, and thrive in a constantly evolving world.

### STORYTIME

When planting a Chinese bamboo seed, it needs proper care, including regular watering, exposure to sunlight, and nutrient-rich soil. Despite all the efforts, no visible growth will be above the ground for the first few years. As a result, the bamboo farmer may worry if anything is happening.

However, something extraordinary happens in the fifth year. The Chinese bamboo tree suddenly rises from the ground, growing as much as 80 feet in just a few weeks. What seemed like a lack of progress for years was a period of significant underground growth and development. The tree's roots spread deep and wide, firmly anchoring it to the ground and preparing it for growth.

"We can learn much about cultivating a growth mindset from the Chinese Bamboo tree."

- **A-** Patience and Persistence: Like the Chinese bamboo tree, growth requires time, patience, and trust. Even when progress is not immediately visible, it's important to keep nurturing our goals and dreams.

- **B-** Trusting the progress: We must trust our journey and efforts, even when results are not immediate. Growth is essential but often invisible.

- **C-** Embracing Growth Mindset: This Chinese bamboo story ultimately embodies the principles of a growth mindset.

Believe in our capacity to grow, persevere through challenges, and embrace setbacks as opportunities for learning and development.

Are there any obstacles to a growth mindset?

People often face obstacles that hinder their growth mindset. There are a few common obstacles

Fixed Mindset Beliefs: Some people may hold fixed beliefs about their abilities or intelligence, leading them to believe that change is impossible and they can not improve.

Can these obstacles be overcome?

Challenging assumptions and embracing effort and learning can lead to growth.

1- Fear Of Failure: Many people avoid taking risks due to the fear of failure. They may also refrain from pursuing challenging goals due to worrying about making mistakes or not meeting expectations. Can they overcome this fear of failure? Encouraging a shift in perspective on failure—as an opportunity for learning and growth—can help you remove this fear and embrace challenges more readily.

2- Negative Self-Talk: Negative self-talk, such as self-doubt or self-criticism, can undermine confidence and resilience, making it challenging to maintain a growth mindset. Positive affirmations, or positive internal dialogue, can help you build resilience and foster a mindset of growth and possibility.

3- Comparison with others: This habit can be dangerous, lowering self-esteem and confidence and making individuals feel inferior. Instead, focusing on personal growth and progress is essential without benchmarking against others.

4- Fixed Mindset Environments: Environments that emphasize performance, competition, and outcomes over effort and growth can reinforce fixed mindset beliefs and hinder the development of a growth mindset.

Create a supportive, nurturing environment that values effort, learning, and improvement. This will help people overcome these obstacles and thrive.

Remember: "By embracing practices that cultivate a growth mindset, you can overcome limiting beliefs and unlock your full potential for growth and success."

### PRACTICAL TIPS TO CULTIVATE A GROWTH MINDSET

**Mindfulness Practices**: Mindfulness techniques, such as meditation and deep breathing exercises, are simple and very effective in cultivating a growth mindset. Mindfulness-based stress reduction can help you develop self-awareness, resilience, and emotional regulation.

**Visualization and Affirmations**: This technique has strong power. Visualize as your goals are already achieved, and use positive affirmations to reinforce your growth mindset.

For example- I embrace challenges as opportunities for growth and learning.

I can overcome any obstacle and achieve my goals with effort and perseverance.

**Gratitude Practice**: Start expressing appreciation for small victories.

**For example**- " I Express Gratitude for the opportunities, experiences, and lessons that contribute to my growth and development."

Incorporate this habit into your daily routine. Practice, and you will feel better.

## GROWTH MINDSET IN ACTION

Alex's Journey of Growth

Alex was a marketing manager in a reputed pharmaceutical company. He was a very ambitious and bright young marketing professional who dreamed of starting his own business. However, after facing investors' rejection and struggling to find his niche in the competitive market, he began questioning his abilities and whether he was cut out for entrepreneurship.

Instead of giving up, Alex adopted a growth mindset and viewed his setbacks as opportunities for learning and growth.

He prepared a list of questions asked by investors and used it as a learning tool. He sought feedback from mentors and industry experts. He invested in learning new skills, and this paid off well.

Despite facing numerous challenges, including financial setbacks and fierce competition, Alex remained resilient and determined to succeed. He learned from each rejection and improved his sales pitch. He continued to improve, and his perseverance and dedication found success. He could get investors. He launched his company, and it is doing well.

Alex's growth mindset enabled him to overcome obstacles, adapt to change, and achieve his dream of becoming a successful entrepreneur.

Remember: "You can unlock your full potential and achieve your goals like Alex. View challenges as opportunities for learning and growth."

### REFLECTION AND ACTION PLANNING

It's crucial to recognize particular patterns of thought and behavior that signify reluctance towards progress and change to spot areas where people might be restricting themselves with a fixed mindset. I want to offer some strategies that can assist in identifying such areas.

1. **Resistance to Change:** People with a fixed mindset are easy to identify. They usually avoid challenging tasks, fearing failure or making mistakes. They may prefer to stick to what they know and are comfortable with rather than taking risks or venturing into unfamiliar territory.

2. **Negative Self-Talk:** Have you heard people say, " I am not good enough?" I'll never be able to do that, or am I not smart/talented, or skilled enough? These are common indicators of a fixed mindset.

3. **Avoidance of feedback:** Observe how people react to feedback. If they become defensive or dismissive, they have a fixed mindset.

4. **Desire for Validation:** Have you ever wondered why some people seek validation or approval from others to validate their worth or abilities? These people have a fixed mindset.

5. **Fear of Failure:** Do you know someone on your team who always seeks perfection? Remember: "Perfection is a glorified version of procrastination." This can prevent people from taking risks or pursuing challenging goals.

By paying attention to specific patterns of thought and behavior, you can gain valuable insights into areas where your team members or colleagues may limit themselves with a fixed mindset. Once you have identified these areas, you can collaborate with them to challenge these self-imposed limitations, promote a growth mindset, and provide them with the support they need to achieve greater resilience, learning, and personal development.

**EXERCISE**

1. Reflect on a recent challenge or setback you encountered. How did you initially perceive this challenge, and how did you respond to it? What lessons did you learn from this experience, and how can you apply them to future challenges?

2. Think about a skill or area of your life where you have previously believed yourself to be limited or lacking. What steps can you take to cultivate a growth-oriented mindset in this area?

3. Consider when you received feedback or criticism, whether personally or professionally. How did you react to this feedback, and what was your internal dialogue? Would you like to change your response in similar situations in the future?

4. Imagine achieving a long-term goal or aspiration that you have set for yourself. What challenges or obstacles do you anticipate encountering along the way, and how might you approach them with a growth mindset? Also, list the resources or support systems you can implement.

5. How can you cultivate gratitude and appreciation for your steps toward your goals? How might this mindset of gratitude contribute to your overall sense of well-being and motivation?

**KEY TAKE-HOME MESSAGES**

1. Embrace Challenges: Challenges are opportunities for growth and learning. Overcoming obstacles is essential to your journey toward personal and professional development.

2. Learn from Feedback: Whether positive or constructive, feedback is valuable information for growth. Approach

feedback with an open mind, seeking to learn and improve rather than seeking validation or approval from others.

3. Cultivate Resilience: Resilience is the ability to bounce back from setbacks and adversity. Cultivate resilience by reframing setbacks as opportunities for learning, maintaining a positive attitude, and trusting in your ability to overcome challenges.

4. Focus on Progress: Not perfection, strive for progress, not perfection, and celebrate your efforts and achievements, whether small or incremental. Remember: Growth is a journey; every step forward brings you closer to your goals.

5. Foster a Growth Mindset: Cultivate a growth mindset by believing in your capacity for growth and embracing the process of learning and improvement. Approach challenges with curiosity, persistence, and a willingness to adapt, knowing that your potential is limitless.

I wish you continued growth and success in your personal and professional life. May you embrace challenges with courage, learn from every experience, and cultivate a mindset of growth and possibility.

We will discuss and learn about time management in the next chapter.

Chapter #5

## MASTERING TIME: "STRATEGIES FOR EFFECTIVE TIME MANAGEMENT"

*"Time is a created thing. To say 'I don't have time,' is liking saying, I don't want to."*

*–Lao Tzu*

**STORYTIME**

Once, there was a young professional, Ramdas, a very committed, honest, and sincere person, a dream of any boss. He struggled to balance work, family, and personal life demands. Despite his best efforts, he often felt overwhelmed and short of time. One day, feeling frustrated and exhausted, Ramdas sought advice from his Guru Ji( Mentor), known for his exceptional time management skills. The mentor ( his Guru Ji) shared his learning journey, which included prioritizing tasks, delegating effectively, and setting boundaries to protect his time. His mentor's wisdom inspired Ramdas to implement new time management strategies daily. Over time, he learned to prioritize tasks, streamline workflow, and create dedicated time for work and personal pursuits. As a result, Ramdas felt more focused, productive, and fulfilled, achieving more excellent balance and success in all areas of his life. His journey gives us a powerful reminder of the transformative impact of effective time management on one's overall well-being and success.

Let us take a few messages from the above story to be an effective time manager-

1. Prioritize Your Time: Identify your most important tasks and allocate time accordingly. Focusing on high-priority activities can maximize your productivity and achieve your goals more effectively. Later in this chapter, we will learn about effective time management methods.

2. Delegation: Delegation is an essential skill for a successful leader. Knowing what to delegate and how to delegate can help you manage your workload and improve team productivity.

3. Set Boundaries: Establishing clear boundaries around your time and energy in your work and personal life is essential. One effective way to set boundaries is to learn to say "No." Saying no to tasks that do not align with your priorities can help you focus on what truly matters.

4. Be Flexible: Being open to adjusting your plans and designing new strategies are essential for effective time management.

5. Practice Self-Care: To stay energized and effective, prioritize self-care and well-being in your time management efforts. How can you practice self-care? Take breaks when needed, prioritize activities that

recharge you, and create space for relaxation during your busy schedule.

Tips to prioritize your time:

Use 80/20 principle. Also known as the Pareto Principle.

1. Identify the Vital Few: The 80/20 principle suggests that roughly 80% of results come from 20% of efforts. Evaluate your tasks and identify the top 20% of your efforts that yield the most significant results.

2. Focus on High-Impact Activities: Look for tasks disproportionately impacting your goals or objectives. These tasks are typically high-value activities that contribute directly to your success or the success of your project.

3. Align with Goals and Priorities: Evaluate each task based on your goals and priorities. Focus on tasks that align closely with your strategies and objectives and contribute to achieving your long-term vision.

4. Eliminate or Delegate Low-Value Tasks: Since you have identified the most important tasks, consider eliminating or delegating lower-priority tasks that do not contribute significantly to your goals. This will help you stay focused on high-impact activities.

Remember: "By applying the 80/20 principle to your task prioritization process, you can focus your time and energy on the activities that deliver the greatest results and move you closer to your objectives."

Let us discuss a few more effective time management techniques:

A. Time Tracking: there are various methods available today to track and analyze how you spend your time. I will share a few of them with you. You will get a fair idea of your current time usage pattern and will identify opportunities for improvement.

B. Time Log: keep a detailed record of activities and tasks throughout the day using a notebook, spreadsheet, or specialized time-tracking software. Note each activity's start and end times and any breaks or interruptions.

C. Time Blocking: Allocate specific blocks of time for different activities or tasks on your calendar. This will help you prioritize essential tasks. Minimizing multitasking allows you to focus on a critical task at a time.

D. Pomodoro Technique: Break work into intervals, typically 25 minutes of focused work followed by a 5-minute short break. Use a timer to track each Pomodoro cycle and take longer breaks after completing a certain number of cycles.

E. Activity Logs: Use an activity log to record your daily activities and assess how you spend your time. Suggestion: Include details like Type of activity, duration, and any associated thoughts or feelings.

**F.** Time-tracking apps: These apps can monitor your daily activities automatically or manually. This tool will help you identify usage patterns.

**G.** Time Audits: Conduct periodic time audits to review your time usage and identify areas for improvement. Analyze your time logs or tracking data to assess your time spent on tasks and activities and identify any inefficiencies or time wasters.

Key Point. "Use tools to gain insights into your digital habits and identify opportunities to reduce distractions and focus on priority tasks."

Remember: "Make well-informed decisions to optimize your productivity and effectiveness".

## Goal Setting and Planning

*"Before anything else, preparation is the key to success."*

*- Alexender Graham Bell*

In the previous episode (my book on Goal Setting), we learned that adjusting action steps is more important than adjusting goals.

Importance of setting SMART goals:

Goal setting provides us with a sense of direction. SMART Goals provide a roadmap for success, ensuring that the objective is Specific, Measurable, Achievable, Relevant, and Time-Bound.

Let me share one example: you can use this relevant method in your field.

SMART Goal:

"Increase monthly sales revenue by 15% within the next six months."

Specific: The goal should be specific, which means what is to be achieved. ( Increase in monthly sales revenue by 15%)

Measurable: Progress toward the goal can be qualified( 15% increase in sales revenue)

Achievable: The goal is realistic and attainable, given current resources and capabilities.

Relevant: The goal aligns with broader business objectives and contributes to overall growth and success.

Time-Bound: A specific time frame is established for achieving the goal( within the next six months)

Action Plan :

We must know current market trends, customer preferences, and competitors' actions. So start with-

**Researching the current market trends.**

This research will help identify potential opportunities to increase sales revenue, such as targeting a new market or launching a new product.

**Set Specific Targets:**

Break down the overall sales revenue goals into monthly targets, for example, a 5% increase per month.

Determine specific sales targets for each product or service category.

**Develop Sales Strategies;**

Develop a comprehensive sales strategy outlining tactics to achieve revenue targets.

Define sales channels, pricing strategies, promotional activities, and sales team targets.

**Implement Marketing Campaigns:**

Launch targeted marketing campaigns to generate leads and drive sales.

Use available channels( of line/online)

Such as social media, email marketing, and events.

**Sales Team Training:**

Provide training and resources to the sales team to improve their selling skills and product knowledge.

Set individual sales targets and incentives and motivate and reward performance.

**Monitor and evaluate Progress**:

Track sales performance against target regularly. You can evaluate revenue, customer conversion rate, and new customer acquisition.

Identify barriers or challenges and make changes in the plan if need be.

"This SMART goal and action plan will provide clear direction and accountability for achieving the desired outcome."

Exercise:

If you are a writer and want to write a book. What will be a

SMART goal for writing a book?

Be Specific and clearly articulate your ( Specific, Measurable, Relevant, and Time-bound) goal for writing the book.

Tips- Keep it simple, Ask yourself Why, know your limits, write down every step, and stay flexible till you set the Goal,

Ask yourself why you want to write this book and what impact you hope it will have. This will help you understand your motivation and keep you focused and committed throughout the writing process.

Remember: "Setting goals is the first step to reaching them."

TIME MANAGEMENT TECHNIQUES

There are various time management techniques available that can be effectively utilized.

**1. The Eisenhower Matrix:**

The Eisenhower Matrix, also known as the Urgent-Important Matrix, allows you to prioritize tasks by urgency and importance.

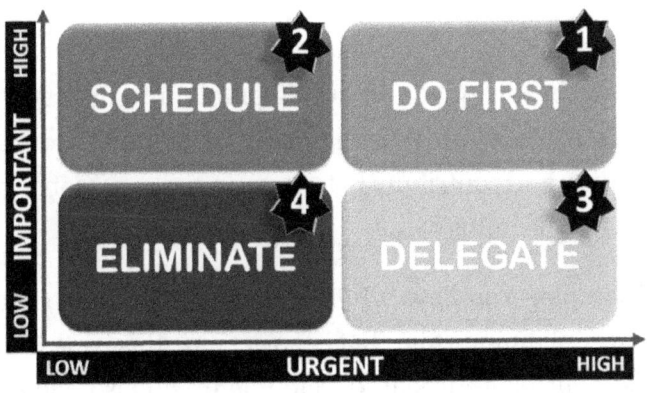

How to use this technique?

This is a powerful tool for prioritizing tasks based on urgency and importance. You can categorize tasks into four quadrants. We will discuss this in detail about how you can focus your time and energy effectively.

**1. Quadrant 1: Urgent and Important- 'Do First'**

Tasks that require immediate attention should be kept in this quadrant as they are both urgent and essential. These tasks are critical and have pressing deadlines or consequences if not completed.

For example, you may have to meet an urgent client request or address a critical issue that may impact your business.

Remember: "Focusing on these tasks first ensures that essential priorities are met and prevents crises from escalating."

**2. Quadrant 2: Important but Not Urgent- 'Schedule'**

Tasks in this quadrant are essential but not urgent. They require proactive planning and scheduling to address effectively and contribute to long-term goals, personal growth, and strategic initiatives.

Example—You have a future project in mind, so you must include planning for that project in this quadrant. An investment plan for skill development will also come in this quadrant. Nurturing key relationships will also feature in this quadrant.

Caution: While these tasks may have few immediate deadlines, neglecting these tasks can lead to missed opportunities or increased stress in the long run.

Remember- "Schedule dedicated time to work on these tasks and ensure they get your attention."

3. **Quadrant 3: Urgent but Not Important- 'Delegate'**

Tasks in this quadrant are urgent but not necessary. They are distractors; they involve interruptions. There may be a minor issue, but it detracts from higher-priority activities.

Example- Today's world is often bombarded with emails and meetings that don't provide value or trivial requests that consume our time.

Caution: While these tasks may demand immediate attention, they do not significantly contribute to long-term goals or essential objectives.

Remember: "Delegate. If you can not delegate, minimize these tasks. Focus on more valuable activities that align with your priorities."

4. **Quadrant 4: Not Urgent and Not Important 'Eliminate'**

Tasks in this quadrant are neither urgent nor essential, representing time-wasting activities, distractions, or low-value tasks.

Example- Browsing social media, engaging in idle gossip, or procrastinating on non-essential tasks.

Caution- while these activities may provide short-term gratification, they do not contribute to productivity, success, or personal fulfillment.

Remember- "Freeing up valuable time and mental energy by minimizing tasks.

**Benefits of using the Eisenhower Matrix:**

Using the Eisenhower Matrix to categorize tasks into these four quadrants, you can gain clarity on your priorities and make informed decisions about where to focus your efforts. You can optimize your productivity and effectiveness in your personal and professional lives.

Let us discuss one more technique for effective time management.

**2. The Two-Minute Rule:**

As per this rule, if a task can be completed in two minutes or less, it should be done immediately rather than postponed or added to a to-do list. The rationale behind this rule is that small tasks often take longer to track and manage than to complete.

This approach will prevent minor tasks from accumulating and cluttering your schedule. You will reduce the tendency to procrastinate.

Following the Two Minute Rule will help make your to-do list smaller and free up mental space.

Remember: "Stay focused on high-value activities that require more time and attention."

## 3. Getting Things Done(GTD) System:

David Allen developed another productivity system called the "Getting Things Done" (GTD).

GTD is a productivity and time management approach that emphasizes putting all tasks, ideas, and commitments into a reliable system, processing them effectively, and taking action systematically.

### FUNDAMENTAL PRINCIPLES OF THE GTD SYSTEM

Capture: collect all incoming tasks, ideas, and commitments into a single inbox or system.

Clarity: Process each item in the inbox and clarify what action needs to be taken. Or no action is required,

Organize: Organize tasks into a context-based list( for example, @ Home,@ Work,@ Errands) and prioritize them based on importance and urgency.

Review: Regularly review and update your lists, projects, and commitments to stay on track and adjust as needed.

Engage: Take action on tasks based on their context, priority, and available resources.

Remember: "The GTD system provides a structured framework for managing tasks and projects, reducing mental clutter, and increasing productivity and focus."

Incorporate these time management techniques to optimize your productivity and success in your personal and professional life while prioritizing effectively.

## CASE STUDY

A professor at a degree college shared a case with me. His son, who was working as a marketing manager at a leading FMCG company, got married during his tenure. Although he was an intelligent and talented marketing brain, his busy schedule and meetings often left him stressed and overwhelmed. He found it challenging to maintain a work-life balance. His father suggested he learn about the Two-Minute Rule, which he decided to try. Whenever he encountered a small task that could be completed in two minutes or less, such as responding to an email or making a quick phone call, he tackled it immediately. As a result, he found that his to-do list became more manageable, and he felt a sense of accomplishment throughout the day. He also learned the art of delegation to get more time for essential tasks. By consistently using the Two-Minute Rule, he soon reclaimed his time and focused on more critical tasks without feeling bogged down by trivial matters. He started enjoying family life in a better way, too.

I suggest practicing the Two-Minute rule, as discussed in this chapter.

## INSIGHT FROM AN EXPERT

John Doe, a productivity coach and author of "Mastering Time Management." Emphasizes the importance of the Two-Minute Rule in optimizing productivity. According to Doe, "Small tasks can quickly pile up and drain your energy if you let them linger on your to-do list. Addressing them promptly with the Two-Minute Rule allows you to create momentum and control your workload. It's a simple yet effective strategy that can significantly impact daily productivity."

## SUMMARY

This chapter explored various techniques and strategies for effective time management. From prioritizing tasks using the Eisenhower Matrix to embracing the Two-Minute Rule, we learned practical methods to optimize productivity and reduce overwhelm. By setting SMART goals, creating action plans, and implementing time-tracking techniques, you can take control of your schedules and achieve greater efficiency. Additionally, we discussed strategies for overcoming common time management obstacles and aligning time management efforts with personal values and priorities.

**"Incorporate these techniques into your daily routines to enhance your productivity and achieve greater success in your personal and professional lives."**

## BUILDING RESILIENT HABITS: SUSTAINING LONG-TERM SUCCESS

Resilient habits are crucial for maintaining momentum and overcoming challenges toward achieving our goals. We will discuss practical tips, valuable insights, and actionable strategies for cultivating resilience and staying motivated long-term. We will discuss in detail the following in the chapter –

- Developing a growth mindset

- Managing setbacks,

- Maintaining consistency and

- Fostering self-care practices.

- Let us travel together to get the best of it.

# Chapter #6

# BUILDING RESILIENT HABITS: SUSTAINING LONG-TERM SUCCESS

*"The oak fought the wind and was broken; the willow bent when it must and survived,"*

*- Robert Jordan*

**STORYTIME**

It was early 1990 when I decided to start a business. I was a sales superstar in my organization and had good savings to start a small business, as shared by Peter, my neighbor in my native city. I launched my business and soon realized it was too early as I had no prior experience and needed to plan better. One chilly evening, as the rain poured outside, my college professor sought shelter in the café. I recognized his face and requested a cup of coffee. Over a cup of hot coffee, I could not control my emotions and expressed my frustration and exhaustion from facing constant challenges in my business venture.

With a gentle smile, my Professor leaned forward and began sharing a story from his family. He recounted when his father faced setbacks and failures in his early years as an entrepreneur. Instead of letting adversity defeat him, he adapted and persevered, learning valuable lessons.

My professor explained how his father cultivated resilient habits, such as maintaining a positive mindset, seeking support from his mentors, and embracing failure as a stepping stone to success. My father likened resilience to the flexibility of a willow tree, which bends with the winds of change but never breaks.

Inspired by my professor's words, I realized that building resilient habits was essential for sustaining long-term success. Armed with renewed determination, I left the café with my professor that day, dropped him off at his residence, and returned with a newfound sense of resilience and optimism, ready to face whatever challenges lay ahead on my journey.

I met Peter after many years and was so happy to see that his business has been going very well and he is having a great time with his sons and grandsons.

Lessons I learned:

One of the most valuable lessons I have learned is resilience's critical role in navigating life's challenges. It's easy to feel overwhelmed when facing obstacles, but developing resilient habits can make all the difference in sustaining long-term success.

Maintaining a resilient mindset means staying flexible in facing adversity like a willow tree, bending with the wind rather than breaking. It's about embracing setbacks as opportunities for growth and finding strength in adversity.

Remember: "Resilience is not just about bouncing back from setbacks; it's about building a foundation of habits that enable us to thrive in the face of adversity."

By cultivating resilience, we empower ourselves to overcome obstacles, stay focused on our goals, and ultimately achieve long-term success.

Let us understand resilience and its importance.

Resilience is a person's capacity to cope with changes and challenges. It is not simply one specific quality; it has multiple factors, including, but not limited to, social support, self–care, and cognitive flexibility.

What is Cognitive flexibility? A person can think about multiple concepts simultaneously.

Cognitive Flexibility- Helps people to handle changes and deal with difficult things.

Remember: "Anyone can be resilient and develop resilience." It is a combination of skills, strategies, and environmental factors. If you practice resilience, you can be resilient.

Life is full of challenges. Today, everyone is stressed, and the atmosphere is full of adversity, so it is essential for us to be resilient to overcome these adversities. Research has proven that resilient people are better at dealing with everyday stress.

## How To Develop Resilience?

Let me share a few strategies to improve your resilience.

### 1. Practice mindfulness

Deep breathing and Yoga help develop resilience. Mindfulness allows us to see our challenges from new perspectives and respond to them more adaptively.

### 2. Create a Reflection Journal

This is a valuable tool for developing resilience and promoting personal growth. How can you create a journal, and how can it help develop resilience?

**A.** Choose a journal format—It can be a physical notebook, a digital journaling app, or an online platform. Choose a format that feels convenient and comfortable for you.

**B.** Dedicate a specific time each day or week for reflection.

**C.** Reflect on experience- Think when you were resilient.

What did you think about the situation?

What did you do?

Now think, If you were not resilient:

What did you do?

What did you think about the situation at that time?

Now, write about challenges you have faced, setbacks you've encountered, and moments of resilience and growth.

What have you learned from these experiences?

### 3. Express emotions

Don't control your emotions; allow yourself to express them freely in your journal. Write about how you felt during difficult times. What emotions do you experience, and how do you cope with them?

### 4. Practice gratitude

Write down things you're grateful for each day, no matter how small. Cultivating gratitude can help shift your focus away from negativity and build resilience.

### 5. Set goals

Set both short-term and long-term goals. Reflect on your progress toward these goals regularly and celebrate your achievements.

Setting and achieving goals will always boost your confidence. So, set realistic goals.

### 6. Practice self-compassion

Be kind to yourself in your journaling practice. Treat yourself with understanding and compassion when you are going through a difficult time. Write self-affirmations and words of encouragement to yourself. For example;

### Self-affirmations:

1. I am capable of overcoming any challenge that comes my way

2. I trust in my ability to adapt and grow in adversity.

3. I believe in myself and my inner strength to persevere through difficult times.

4. I choose to focus on the positive aspects of my life and let go of negativity.

5. I am deserving of respect and kindness, both from myself and others.

**Words of encouragement:**

1. Keep going, even when it feels tough, you have got this!

2. Remember how far you've come and all the obstacles you've overcome.

3. You are stronger and more resilient than you realize; believe in yourself.

4. Every setback is an opportunity for growth and learning. Embrace it.

5. Be kind to yourself and treat yourself with the same compassion you offer others.

6. Take one step at a time, and celebrate every small victory.

7. Trust in the journey, and believe everything will work out toward the end.

## Storytime

Walt Sisney's Story of Resilience:

Walt Disney, the visionary behind one of the most iconic brands in the world, faced numerous challenges on his journey to success. In the early days of his career, Disney experienced multiple failures and setbacks. His first animation studio went bankrupt and was even rejected by banks for loans to fund his creative projects. Can you believe that he faced 300 Rejections from financiers? Despite that, Disney remained undeterred. He continued to believe in his vision of creating a magical world of animation that would capture the hearts of audiences around the globe. Disney did not allow failure to discourage him; he used it as fuel to propel himself forward. He adapted to adversity, innovated in the face of challenges, and persisted in pursuing his dreams.

With the power of his resilience and determination, Disney eventually founded the Walt Disney Company, forever changing the entertainment landscape.

His creations: ' Beloved characters like "Mickey Mouse" and the iconic film "Snow White and Seven Dwarfs" have left an indelible mark on generations of audiences.

Key takeaways:

Walt Disney's story reminds us that resilience is essential for overcoming obstacles and achieving success.

Staying committed to our goals, we can sustain success over the long term, no matter what challenges we may face.

Remember: 'By building resilient habits and staying true to our dreams, we can overcome adversity and create a legacy that inspires others for generations to come.'

## SOME TIPS FOR BUILDING RESILIENCE

As we know, each individual and their needs are unique. Different things will work for different people, but I will share some of my ideas with you to try.

1. Develop and maintain strong relationships: Having a support system of friends, family, and mentors can provide invaluable emotional support during difficult times.

2. Turn setbacks into opportunities: Resilient people view setbacks as opportunities for growth and learning. They adapt to challenges and use them as stepping stones toward future success.

3. Develop a positive outlook: Maintaining a positive mindset can help individuals overcome adversity more quickly.

4. Remember, "Optimism and resilience go hand in hand."

5. Take care of yourself: Physical and mental well-being are essential for resilience; prioritizing self-care activities, such as exercise, healthy eating, and stress management, can bolster resilience.

6. Find ways to help others: Giving back can provide a sense of purpose and fulfillment while fostering social connections and resilience.

These tips will help you build resilience, from interpersonal relationships to self-care and community engagement.

If you are working as a Sales Leader, then I would also like to suggest a few more strategies ;

1. **Effective communication techniques:** Selling is a noble profession. It's more than just closing deals or meeting their daily work quota. It is about forging meaningful connections, solving problems, and creating value for customers and businesses. In the sales world, success isn't measured in dollars and cents but in your positive impact on people's lives. Remember: As a sales leader, you can inspire, influence, and uplift those around you.

2. **Cultivate empathy and understanding:** Take the time to truly understand your customers' needs, challenges, and aspirations. By empathizing with their situation, you can tailor your approach and offerings to provide genuine solutions that resonate with them.

3. **Lead with integrity and honesty:** Trust is the foundation of any successful sales relationship. Always prioritize honesty, transparency, and integrity in your interactions with customers and colleagues. Your reputation as a trustworthy sales leader will precede you and open doors to new opportunities.

4. **Embrace Continuous Learning and Improvement:** The sales landscape constantly evolves, and successful sales leaders are committed to lifelong learning and growth. Stay curious, seek out new knowledge and skills, and be willing to adapt your approach in response to changing market dynamics.

5. **Foster a culture of collaboration and teamwork:** Sales is a team sport, and your success as a leader depends on the collective efforts of your team members. Cultivate a culture of collaboration, mutual support, and shared goals where everyone feels valued and empowered to contribute their best.

6. **Stay resilient and focused:** Sales can be a challenging and demanding profession, but it's also rewarding. Stay resilient in the face of setbacks, maintain a positive mindset, and stay focused on your long-term goals.

**Remember:** 'Every rejection is just a stepping stone to success.'

Believe: you can elevate yourself and your team to new heights of success and fulfillment. Together, let's redefine what it means to be a sales leader and make a lasting impact on the world.

## REAL-LIFE SUCCES STORY: MONA'S JOURNEY TO SALES EXCELLENCE

Meet Mona, a dedicated sales professional who embodies the noble qualities of her profession—starting her career in sales with no experience and out of compulsion. Mona lost his father early and was needed to support her mother and two younger siblings. Mona faced numerous challenges and setbacks along the way. Her dedication to ethical sales practices, determination to be a sales superstar, and commitment to her customers set her apart from her peers,

Early in her career, Mona encountered a difficult situation in which her manager pressured her to meet aggressive sales targets at the expense of customer trust. Despite the pressure, Mona prioritized integrity and honesty in her client interactions. She always took the time to listen to her customers' needs and concerns and offer solutions that genuinely benefited them, even if it meant sacrificing short-term gains.

Mona's approach paid off in the long run. One of her prominent clients recommended her name to a giant company, and she was selected there. She built a reputation for reliability, professionalism, and genuine care for her clients' success. Her satisfied customers not only became loyal repeat buyers but also referred new business to her through word–of–mouth recommendations.

As her career progressed, she continued to hone her skills and expand her knowledge through ongoing education and professional development. Her company sponsored her MBA, and she was nominated to attend many industry conferences. By investing in her growth, Mona could stay ahead of the curve and maintain her competitive edge in the market.

Today, Mona is regarded as a top-performing sales professional in her industry. She consistently exceeds sales targets, earns accolades from her clients and colleagues, and is a role model for aspiring professionals. Many management schools invite her to motivate their students. For those students, she is a role model. She takes pride in knowing her success is built on integrity, trust, and genuine customer care.

**KEY TAKE-HOME MESSAGES**

Mona's ability to overcome personal and professional challenges highlights the importance of resilience.

Mona's willingness to adapt to changing circumstances made her thrive in a dynamic environment and capitalize on emerging opportunities.

Remember- "Believe in yourself, persevere through challenges, and watch as your dreams become your reality."

Summary:

This chapter explored the importance of resilience in navigating life's challenges and sustaining long-term success. Through real-life examples and practical insights, we learned how resilience enables people to overcome adversity and thrive in dynamic environments. From developing resilient habits to embracing change and adapting to new opportunities, we discovered the power of self-belief and perseverance in achieving our goals. By cultivating a growth mindset, prioritizing self-care, and finding ways to help others, we empower ourselves to navigate life's ups and downs with confidence and courage. Building resilience is not just about bouncing back from setbacks but about thriving in the face of adversity, turning obstacles into opportunities, and unlocking our full potential.

Life presents many twists and turns. We need to have strategies to overcome them. Welcome to the journey of navigating challenges.

Chapter #7

## NAVIGATING CHALLENGES: STRATEGIES FOR ADAPTABILITY AND FLEXIBILITY

*"The only way to make sense of change is to plunge into it, move with it, and join the dance."*

*- Alan Walts*

The world is changing quickly today, full of uncertainties and surprises. Challenges and uncertainties are inevitable in both personal and professional life. Today, there is a need for adaptability and flexibility. Unexpected obstacles can derail even the best-laid plans. However, embracing adaptability and flexibility can weather these storms and thrive amidst change and uncertainty. Let us explore the key strategies and insights to help you navigate challenges effectively. Empowering you to embrace change, seize opportunities, and achieve your goals.

Let us understand the adaptability and flexibility :

Adaptability involves foresight and proactive planning to prepare for potential challenges, whereas flexibility is more responsive and adaptable at the moment, often requiring the accommodation of others. Any employer will value both qualities as they enable a dynamic and agile work environment that effectively navigates transition and unexpected changes.

## Importance Of Adaptability And Flexibility

Adaptability is a cornerstone trait essential for success in both personal and professional spheres. Being adaptable means having the flexibility to adjust to various situations, navigate life's ups and downs, and thrive in uncertainty. Whether it's adapting to changes in relationships, health, or life circumstances, anyone who possesses adaptability is better equipped to handle challenges and bounce back from setbacks.

Similarly, adaptability is equally crucial in the professional realm. With the rapid pace of technological advancements, market shifts, and organizational changes, professionals must be agile and adaptable to stay relevant and competitive. Those who demonstrate adaptability can quickly pivot in response to evolving industry trends, embrace new technologies and methodologies, and effectively collaborate with diverse teams.

Moreover, adaptability fosters innovation and problem-solving abilities in the workplace. Look around your workplace, and you will notice a few people who are open to change and experimentation and are more likely to generate creative solutions, identify new opportunities, and drive organizational growth.

In short :

Adaptability emphasizes the ability to evolve and adjust over time, while flexibility focuses on the agility and responsiveness needed to navigate immediate changes or demands. Both traits are valuable in personal and professional life, complementing each other to foster resilience, innovation, and success in an ever-changing world.

Remember: 'Today, adaptability is not just a desirable trait but a fundamental skill that empowers us to thrive amidst uncertainty and complexity.'

## ROLE OF GROWTH MINDSET IN FOSTERING ADAPTABILITY AND FLEXIBILITY

Adapting and remaining flexible has become increasingly crucial in today's fast-paced world. Let me share the story.

### STORYTIME

One of my friends, David, is a seasoned marketing manager working with a leading healthcare company. He faced a sudden shift in his industry's landscape. With the rise of digital marketing platforms, traditional marketing strategies were becoming obsolete, presenting him with a daunting challenge. Instead of resisting change, David recognized the need to adapt his approach to meet the evolving demands of his field.

David began by embracing continuous learning, immersing himself in online courses and workshops to familiarize himself with emerging marketing friends and technologies. He also cultivated a growth mindset, viewing setbacks as opportunities for growth rather than insurmountable obstacles. When his company implemented new software to streamline marketing processes, David eagerly embraced the change, taking the lead in training his team and exploring innovative ways to leverage the technology.

However, more than adaptability alone was needed to navigate the complexities of David's evolving industry. Flexibility played a crucial role in his success and allowed him to pivot quickly in response to shifting priorities and unforeseen challenges. When a critical marketing campaign faced unexpected delays due to budget constraints, David demonstrated flexibility by reallocating resources and adjusting timelines without sacrificing quality or impact. His ability to remain agile in the face of uncertainty ensured that his team remained focused, motivated, and ultimately successful.

**KEY LEARNINGS FROM DAVID'S EXPERIENCE**

Embrace Change: David embraced change rather than resisting it. By recognizing the need to evolve with the times, you can position yourself for success in a rapidly shifting world.

Continuous Learning: David's commitment to continuous learning underscores the value of staying informed about emerging trends and technologies. By investing in ongoing education and skill development. You can remain competent and relevant in your field.

Growth Mindset: David's ability to view setbacks as opportunities for growth demonstrates the power of a growth mindset. By reframing challenges as learning experiences and maintaining a positive outlook, you can overcome obstacles and achieve your goals.

Agility and Resilience: David's agility and resilience in uncertainty highlight the importance of remaining flexible and adaptable. You can pivot quickly in response to changing circumstances by staying agile and resilient.

Remember: "Navigate challenges and seize opportunities effectively."

**PRACTICAL TIPS TO INCORPORATE FLEXIBILITY INTO DAILY ROUTINES AND DECISION-MAKING PROCESSES**

1- Embrace Uncertainty: Accept that change is inevitable and be open to adapting plans and strategies as circumstances evolve.

2- Stay Agile: Cultivate an agile mindset by remaining receptive to new information and adjusting your approach accordingly.

3- Make Adaptability a priority: Align your goals, strategies, and priorities with changing needs and circumstances.

4- Practice Mindfulness: Develop self-awareness and emotional intelligence to understand your reactions and responses to change for the better. Be more adaptable.

5- Foster a culture of flexibility: Encourage flexibility and innovation within your team or organization by promoting open communication, collaboration, and a willingness to experiment with new ideas and approaches.

6- Be open to feedback: Solicit feedback from others to gain different perspectives and insights. This will help you identify blind spots and make more informed decisions.

And feel free to try new things and experiment with different approaches, even if they involve some risk. Even if you fail, failure can still be a valuable experience that will lead to growth and innovation.

Inevitably, you will encounter new opportunities and pathways for growth. One such avenue lies in the power of connections. Expanding your sphere of influence through networking and building meaningful relationships can enhance your adaptability and open doors to new opportunities and collaboration. Let's explore how cultivating connections can empower you to thrive in an ever-changing world.

## Chapter #8

# EXPANDING YOUR SPHERE OF INFLUENCE: THE POWER OF CONNECTIONS

*"Your network is your net worth."*

*- Porter Gale*

According to Chanakya, networking involves cultivating connections with influential individuals, peers, and stakeholders to garner support, exchange information, and leverage collective resources for mutual benefit.

**About Chanakya:** An ancient Indian teacher, philosopher, economist, and royal advisor.

**His strategic networking and diplomatic skills played a crucial role in shaping the political landscape of ancient India**, as he forged alliances with various rulers and kingdoms to establish the Maurya empire under Chandragupta Maurya's reign.

In today's business world, we often see people working to strengthen their networking and create new business opportunities for collaboration and relationship building. Networking is also helpful in career advancement.

### HOW CAN YOU IMPROVE NETWORKING?

Let us discuss a few tips-

1- **Be Genuine:** Build genuine connections based on mutual interest and shared values rather than solely focusing on self-promotion. Be sincere in your approach.

2- **Listen Actively:** Practice active listening during conversations to understand others' perspectives and needs. Show genuine interest in their experiences and expertise.

3- **Add Values:** Offer assistance, insights, or resources that can benefit others without expecting immediate returns. This will strengthen relationships and will foster trust.

4- **Diversify Connections:** Seek networking opportunities beyond your immediate industry or social circle. Attend different events, join professional groups, and engage with people from diverse backgrounds and industries.

5- **Follow-up:** This is the key; some people need to remember the event and the people they met at these events. Follow up with contacts to express gratitude, share relevant information, or schedule future interactions. Consistent communication helps maintain connections over time.

6- **Use Social Media Platforms** to showcase your expertise, connect with professionals in your field, and stay updated on industry trends. LinkedIn is one such platform.

7- Attend Networking Events: Actively participate in networking events, conferences, seminars, and workshops to expand your network and meet new contacts face-to-face.

Remember: 'You can enhance your networking skills and leverage connections to support your personal and professional growth.'

**NETWORKING ACTION PLAN**

**1.** Identify networking Goals: write down your networking objectives.

Are you looking to expand your professional contacts? Are you Seeking Mentorship, exploring new career opportunities, or something else? Remember: Be specific while writing your goal.

**2.** Revisit your Current Network: who are your existing contacts?

They belong to which Industry or field?

Remember - 'Once you are done, Identify any gaps or areas of improvement.'

Create a Networking Strategy: what action can you take to expand your network? For example-

I will attend industry events, seminars, workshops, and networking events relevant to my field.

I will leverage online platforms such as LinkedIn and industry-specific online communities.

I will join and attend professional forums.

I will seek mentorship and guidance.

I will offer my support and help to others.

Remember: 'Helping others will help you to attract more meaningful connections.'

I learned the importance of **networking** from my father. My father was my first mentor, coach, and guide when I was a young boy. He was also my first teacher. He taught me many lessons, and I am happy to share one meeting with him and Ramdas. ( Do you Remember Ramads? He is our companion in this journey right from episode No.1—The One Thing—' That Will Make You an Effective Leader.')

Ramdas came late that day and had many questions in his mind. His first question was, What is most important for success?

My father responded with a smile on his face- **Self-discipline**! I thought Ramdas was trying to teach him a lesson since he was late, but later, I learned he was severe and continued. He said, Look, Ramada, Self Discipline is the foundation for success. You can control your emotions, and self-discipline will help you focus on your goals. You will make well-informed decisions and will consistently achieve long-term success.

There were many other points for discussion, and I interrupted many times with my little understanding and confusion. My father taught us another important lesson that day. He said if you want to succeed, you must be ready to be a lifelong learner.

He advised us with his timeless wisdom, "Information is the key to success." Later in life, I realized we must gain knowledge from various sources and keep ourselves updated with the latest trends.

His advice was to read books and invest in self-development.

My other Learning from that discussion is to think Big but be **strategic** in your **thinking**. His suggestion to us was simple- analyze the situation and understand the strengths and weaknesses of your competitors. ( I remember this was in the context of winning a football match with another village)

His simple advice was- to assess risks, identify opportunities, and make well-thought-out decisions to achieve a desired outcome or planned success.

He continued to teach us with examples. If your goal is to win the match, then be ready to accept that there will be challenges, obstacles, and failures at times, but you should have a **never-give-up attitude.** He always encourages us to remain determined and focused on winning the game of life.

My other learning was that networking and alliances are essential for achieving success. Networking with like-minded people, collaborating with others, and forming alliances can mutually benefit all parties involved.

Ramdas pointed out that a player's foul cost them a match point in the last match. Learning came as Ethical conduct. Unethical means to achieve success are short-lived. There is no substitute for honesty and integrity. Follow ethical principles to build trust. And then he looked at Ramdas and said, 'Time Management.' There was silence for some time, and my father took the initiative to continue. Always value the need for effective time management.

Remember- "Time wasted is an opportunity lost."

Set realistic goals

Allocate time to each goal based on its merit( priority)

Remember- Following these principles will accomplish more, meet deadlines, and progress toward your goals.

Let us summarize:

This chapter explored the significance of expanding one's sphere of influence through networking and building connections. We discussed how networking can open doors to new opportunities, enhance career growth, and foster personal development. By sharing practical tips, strategies, and real-life examples, we learned the importance of self-discipline, time management, Goal setting, and prioritization. Additionally, we highlighted the value of alliances and their role in expanding our reach and influence.

"**Strengthen your network and maximize your potential.**"

Having explored the power of connections in expanding our sphere of influence, we now focus on another crucial aspect of personal and professional growth: continuous learning; just as connections open doors to new opportunities, embracing a mindset of lifelong learning fuels our journey toward success.

# Chapter #9

## EMBRACING CONTINUOUS LEARNING: FUELING PERSONAL AND PROFESSIONAL GROWTH

*"Education is the kindling of a flame, not the filling of a vessel."*

*- Socrates*

Let me continue with the interaction between My Father and Ramdas. With Guru Ji's permission, Ramdas asked how knowledgeable he had become. Guru Ji replied, "Ramdas, knowledge is like the ocean, vast and boundless. Just as a river continuously flows and adds to the ocean, so should your quest for learning. Never be satisfied with what you know, for there is always more to discover and explore."

I remember his last sentence, he said, Ramdas," What you know is important, and rest is more important." So, continue to learn more and develop a mindset that will help you be a lifelong learner.

Daily habits and practices for the foundation of continuous learning. You can learn from anyone; you can learn in formal or informal setups. It can be theoretical, practical, or knowledge or skill set.

In continuous learning, team members retain knowledge and skills over time.

## WHY CONTINUOUS LEARNING MATTERS FOR THE BUSINESS

Organizations increasingly prioritize workshops, training sessions, and outbound programs for their employees, recognizing the significance of continuous learning. As the adage goes, '**Knowledge is power**.' Well-trained employees possess the expertise and skills to contribute to their organizations' success significantly.

"**Cost-effective**" – Recognizing the high cost associated with recruitment and turnover, organizations understand the importance of investing in their existing talent pool. By prioritizing employee development initiatives, they mitigate the risks of turnover and the expenses incurred in hiring and onboarding new employees. Moreover, fostering continuous learning opportunities ensures employees remain engaged, motivated, and committed to achieving organizational goals.

Continuous learning initiatives demonstrate that employees are **highly valued** within the organization. By investing in their professional development, the organization communicates a genuine commitment to nurturing talent and fostering career growth. This support enhances employee morale and engagement and cultivates a culture of learning and innovation, ultimately driving organizational success.

## THE VALUE OF CONTINOUS LEARNING FOR LEADERS

Let us discuss a few benefits-

**Adaptability-** Continuous learning helps leaders stay adaptable in a rapidly changing business environment, equipping them with the knowledge and skills to navigate new challenges effectively.

**Innovation-** By fostering a culture of continuous learning, leaders inspire innovation within their teams. They are likelier to explore new ideas and approaches, driving creativity and problem-solving.

**Leadership Development-** Continuous learning contributes to ongoing leadership development by expanding leaders' perspectives, enhancing their decision-making abilities, and fostering self-awareness and emotional intelligence.

**Employee Engagement—Leaders** prioritizing continuous learning set a positive example for their teams, encouraging employees to invest in their growth and development. This leads to higher levels of employee engagement and retention.

**Organizational Success-** Ultimately, the value of continuous learning for leaders lies in its impact on organizational success. Leaders who embrace learning contribute to a culture of growth and improvement, driving innovation, fostering employee development, and ultimately driving the organization toward goals.

## PRACTICAL TIPS FOR CONTINUOUS LEARNING

1. **Set Clear Goals-** Define your learning objectives and identify specific skills or knowledge areas you want to develop; setting clear goals will help you stay focused and motivated. For example- you want to complete an online certification course in social media marketing within the next six months.

2. **Create a Learning Plan-**Develop a structured learning plan that outlines how you will achieve your goals. Break down your learning objectives into smaller, manageable tasks and create a timeline for completion. For example, if you want to develop expertise in cloud compounding, break it down into smaller tasks, like reading relevant books, watching video tutorials, and completing hands-on experiences.

3. **Utilize Various Learning Resources-** Explore various learning resources, including online courses, books, podcasts, webinars, and workshops. Choose formats that suit your learning style and preferences.

4. **Allocate Regular Time for Learning-**Schedule dedicated time for learning activities in your calendar regularly. Treat learning as a priority and commit to investing time in personal and professional development.

5. **Stay Curious and Open-Minded-** Cultivate a mindset of curiosity and open-mindedness. Be willing

to explore new ideas, perspectives, and approaches, and embrace opportunities to learn from others.

6. **Seek Feedback and Reflection—Seek feedback on your progress and performance from peers, mentors, or seniors.** Reflect on your learning experiences, identify areas for improvement, and adjust your approach as needed.

7. **Apply Leaning to Real-Life Situations-** Look for opportunities to apply what you have learned to real-life situations in your work or personal life. Practice implementing new skills or knowledge to reinforce learning and deepen understanding.

8. **Collaborate and Share Knowledge-** Engage in collaborative learning activities with colleagues or peers. Please share your knowledge and expertise with others, and be open to learning from their experiences and insights.

9. **Track Your Progress—Track** your learning progress and accomplishments. Celebrate milestones and achievements along the way to stay motivated and inspired.

10. **Stay Updated and Adapt-** Stay informed about emerging trends, developments, and advancements in your field. Continuously update your skills and knowledge to remain relevant and adaptable in a rapidly changing world.

Remember: 'Continuous learning begins with Leaders.'

Leaders who prioritize continuous learning set a positive example for their teams, promoting a culture of growth and development.

Continuous learning empowers leaders to stay ahead of the curve and drive meaningful change within their teams and organizations.

Conclusion:

Continuous learning is not just a destination but a lifelong journey of growth and development. By embracing curiosity, resilience, and a passion for learning, you can unlock your full potential and thrive personally and professionally.

Reflect on how you can integrate continuous learning into their daily routines and commit to ongoing personal and professional development.

Together, let us embark on this journey of discovery and growth, empowered to create positive change and achieve our fullest potential.

Acknowledging the hard work done by your team members not only boosts morale but also reinforces a sense of value and belonging with the Organization.

Some leaders understand the power of celebrating their team's success, no matter how small. Recognizing the importance of breaking significant goals into smaller, achievable milestones, it becomes crucial to recognize and celebrate each step of progress. These celebrations are tangible expressions of appreciation and recognition for our team members' tireless efforts and valuable contributions.

Join me as we explore the profound impact of celebrating milestones on teams. Discover how these celebrations can serve as powerful motivators, inspiring individuals to persevere and excel in their personal and professional pursuits.

## Chapter #10

## CELEBRATING MILESTONES: RECOGNIZING PROGRESS AND STAYING MOTIVATED

*"Success is not just about reaching the destination, but also about acknowledging and celebrating the journey along the way."*

*- Unknown*

I am sharing an Inspiring success story of Mrs. Rajni Bector, the Chairperson of Bectors Food Specialities Ltd.

In the busy streets of Ludhiana in Punjab state, there was a small bakery run by the Bector family. Mrs.Bector began her journey as a businesswoman in 1970 by crafting homemade delicacies like icecreams, pudding, cakes, coolies, and buns for local celebrations. Despite a humble beginning, her passion for baking and commitment to quality soon generated attention beyond the borders of her hometown.

Mrs. Bector's relentless drive and unwavering dedication [ropelled her small venture to remarkable heights. With an initial investment of just Rs 20,000 ( 240 Dollars), she laid the foundation for Mrs. Bector's Food Specialities Ltd, a renowned name in biscuits and bakery products.

1985, the first milestone of Mrs. Bector's extraordinary success was reached as she established a bread unit in Punkab, churning out 5000 loaves daily. The overwhelming response from customers spurred her to expand tenfold, producing an impressive 50,000 loaves daily.

With each passing year, Mrs Bector's empire continued to flourish. From supplying burger buns to McDonald's in 1996 to introducing popular brands like Cremica and Nournbon, her company's footprint grew exponentially. Today, products under the Cremica, Bourbon, and English Oven brands grace shelves in over twenty-three states across India, available through a vast network of 550,000 outlets.

2020 marked another milestone in Mrs. Bector's illustrious journey as her company launched its IPO, oversubscribed by a staggering 198 times, raising Rs 541 Crore( 5.4 Billion). This monumental success catapulted the company's market cap to a staggering Rs.6681 Crore ( 668.1 Billion)

Mrs. Rajni Bector's remarkable achievements have not gone unnoticed. Honored with the Padma Shri award( the fourth highest civilian award of the Republic of India), she stands as a beacon of inspiration, proving that extraordinary success is within reach with passion, perseverance, and unwavering belief in one's dreams. Her journey from a humble home kitchen to the global business stage is a testament to the power of resilience and determination.

We have many takeaways from Mrs Bector's Specialities foods Journey-

**Acknowledge Every Achievement**- Celebrate even small wins to maintain morale and momentum.

**Create a Positive Culture-** Foster an environment where employees feel valued and appreciated for their contributions.

**Fuel Motivation-** Recognizing progress boosts motivation and inspires teams to strive for more tremendous success.

**Build Team Spirit-** Celebrating milestones together strengthens bonds and promotes collaboration.

**Stay Focused on the Journey-** Enjoying the journey and celebrating progress is as important as reaching the destination.

Mrs Bector Specialities Foods' story reminds us of the transformative power of celebrating milestones.

Remember: 'By recognizing achievements along the way, you can inspire greater dedication, foster a positive work culture, and propel yourself towards success.'

## SOME TIPS TO CELEBRATE THE MILESTONES AND SUCCESS

In my experience, celebrating milestones has been a meaningful and rewarding practice. One of my favorite ways to commemorate achievements is by treating myself to something special, like purchasing a book from my favorite author and inscribing the occasion and date on the first page. These books serve as constant reminders of my journey and provide ongoing motivation. Additionally, I prioritize expressing my gratitude and appreciation to my team members by sending handwritten letters to celebrate their success. This personal touch fosters a sense of connection and recognition within the team. Furthermore, I believe in sharing our success with loved ones, so I always call friends and family members to share the joy of our achievements.

### REFLECTION QUESTION

Reflect on a recent milestone or success in your life.

How did you celebrate it, and how did that celebration make you feel?

What did you learn from that experience?

### EXERCISE

Write down three milestones or successes you hope to achieve in the next 12 months.

For each one, brainstorm three unique and meaningful ways to celebrate when you reach it.

These celebrations can be big or small, but focus on making them personal and meaningful to you.

Before we say goodbye with best wishes, let me share the core principles covered in this book:

1. **Apparent Goals Drive Success:** Setting clear, actionable goals is the foundation for success.

2. **Resilience is Key:** Resilience allows leaders to overcome obstacles, adapt to change, and persevere through challenges,

3. **Adaptability Fuels Growth:** Embracing adaptability enables leaders to navigate uncertainty and capitalize on new opportunities.

4. **Continuous Learning Drives Excellence:** Committing to lifelong learning fosters personal and professional growth, enhancing leadership effectiveness.

5. **Networking Strengthens Connections:** Building strong networks fosters collaboration, support, and opportunities for growth and development.

6. **Celebrating Milestones Motivates:** Recognizing achievements boosts morale, fosters a positive culture, and reinforces progress toward goals.

7. **Effective Communication Builds Trust:** Clear, transparent communication fosters trust, alignment, and engagement among team members.

8. **Empowering Others Drives Success:** Empowering team members fosters ownership, accountability, and innovation, driving collective success.

9. **Strategic Planning Guides Action. It provides direction, focus, and alignment, ensuring that** efforts are purposeful and impactful.

10. **Vision and Values Guide Leadership.** Aligning actions with a clear vision and core values instills purpose, direction, and integrity in leadership.

**Now that we have covered our basics, it's time to implement them. Before we bid farewell, always remember:**

*"Success is not the key to happiness; Happiness is the key to success. If you love what you are doing, you will be successful."* = Albert Schweitzer

### STORYTIME

One day, Ramdas asked his Guru Ji, " Guru Ji, how can I achieve success?" We all have this question in our minds. Sometimes, we hesitate to ask, and sometimes, we don't know whom to ask. Do you agree?

With a smile, Guru Ji replied," Success is like a Fruit Tree. Plant the seed of hard work, nurture it with determination, and water it with persistence. In time, you will harvest the fruits of your hard work."

My best Wishes for great success in your life:

*"As you embark on your journey to success, remember the wisdom of the ages. Embrace challenges as opportunities, cultivate resilience in adversity, and never lose sight of your goals. Dedication, perseverance, and a belief in your potential can achieve greatness in every aspect of your life.*

*Trust yourself, stay true to your values, and let the light of wisdom and inspiration guide your journey."*

**With warm Regards,**

J P Pathak

# ABOUT THE AUTHOR

JP Pathak emerges as a seasoned professional in sales, management, training, and coaching, with a remarkable journey spanning over 35 years. As a dedicated student of sales and management, he has honed his expertise as a practitioner and mentor, guiding individuals to discover their "One Thing" that propels them toward realizing their dreams and purpose.

Throughout his extensive career, JP has navigated the intricacies of sales and marketing, earning a reputation as a sales superstar.

One of JP's distinctive qualities lies in his ability to simplify complex concepts, making them accessible and understandable for his audience. His training and coaching methods are infused with humor, creating an environment that fosters relaxation and comfort, even in challenging situations or when dealing with difficult-to-manage individuals.

JP's effectiveness as a trainer is not solely based on his vast experience but is enriched by his capacity to weave anecdotes and small stories into his teachings. These narratives serve as memorable lessons, ensuring that the knowledge imparted remains ingrained in the minds of his students for an extended period.

JP imparts wisdom and creates an engaging and enjoyable learning experience by incorporating humor and storytelling.

Beyond his professional endeavors, JP Pathak is a science graduate who shares his life with his wife and two daughters. His commitment extends beyond individual growth, as he actively contributes to developing people and organizations. Through his training and coaching initiatives, JP leaves an indelible mark on the journey of those he guides, fostering growth and success.

# Other Books Written By The Author

**Click this book**

**Click this book**

**Click this book**

**Click this book**

**Click this book**

# Disclaimer

This book is for informational purposes only. Readers acknowledge that the author does not render legal, financial, medical, or professional advice. The content within this book has been derived from various sources. Please consult a licensed professional before attempting any techniques outlined in this book.

By reading this document, the reader agrees that under no circumstances is the author responsible for any direct or indirect losses incurred due to the use of the information contained within this document, including but not limited to errors, omissions, or inaccuracies. Adherence to all applicable laws and regulations, including international, federal, state, and local governing professional licensing, business practices, advertising, and all other jurisdictions, is the sole responsibility of the purchaser or reader. Neither the author nor the publisher assumes any responsibility or liability on behalf of the purchaser or reader of these materials. Any perceived slight of any individual or organization is purely unintentional.

# May I Ask You A Favor?

First, I want to say a big thanks for reading this book. You could have chosen any other book, but you took mine, and I appreciate this. I hope you have a few actionable insights that can positively impact your daily life.

Can I ask for 30 seconds more of your time?

I'd love it if you could leave a review of the book. That will help me grow my readership by encouraging folks to take a chance on my books.

**Keeping it straight - *reviews are the lifeblood of any author.***

It will take less than a minute of your time but will tremendously help me reach out to more people. **Kindly provide your review at the store you bought this book from.** And I'd love to see your review. Thanks for your support.

www.ingramcontent.com/pod-product-compliance
Lightning Source LLC
Chambersburg PA
CBHW070250230526
45470CB00002B/549